Teaching English Writing

by Anita Pincas

Essential Language Teaching Series

General Editor: Monica Vincent, Roger H Flavell

 MODERN ENGLISH PUBLICATIONS

First published 1982
Reprinted 1989, 1991

Published by *Macmillan Publishers Ltd*
London and Basingstoke

ISBN 0–333–29312–6

Typeset by Santype International Ltd., Salisbury
Printed in Hong Kong

Contents

Introduction   vii

PART ONE   THE WRITING LESSON   1

1   Starting to prepare a writing lesson   2
1.1   Teaching aims   2
1.2   Integrating writing into a course   5
1.3   Teaching method   13

PART TWO   WRITING SKILLS   25
Introduction   26

2   Communication   28
2.1   Communication between people   28
2.1.1   Classroom application   30
2.2   Suiting a specific subject   32
2.2.1   Classroom application   33
2.3   Presenting ideas   36
2.3.1   Classroom application   43

3 Composition 45

3.1	Sentences	45
3.1.1	Classroom application	47
3.2	Paragraphs	50
3.2.1	Classroom application	54
3.3	Linking devices (cohesion)	55
3.3.1	Classroom application	59

4 Style 63

4.1	The four major styles	63
4.1.1	Classroom application	64
4.2	Formality	66
4.2.1	Classroom application	67
4.3	Emotive tone	69
4.3.1	Classroom application	70

PART THREE	WRITING EXERCISES	73
Introduction		74

5 Familiarisation 78

5.1	General principles	78
5.2	Familiarisation by identifying	79
5.2.1	Identifying by underlining	80
5.2.2	Identifying by matching	81
5.2.3	Identifying by comparing	83
5.2.4	Identifying by multiple choice questions	85
5.2.5	Identifying by re-ordering	86
5.2.6	Identifying by using plans and outlines	87
5.3	Familiarisation by evaluating	87
5.3.1	Evaluating by underlining	87
5.3.2	Evaluating by matching	88
5.3.3	Evaluating by comparing	88
5.3.4	Evaluating by multiple choice questions	89

| 5.3.5 | Evaluating by re-ordering | 89 |
| 5.3.6 | Evaluating by correcting/improving | 90 |

6 Controlled writing 91

6.1	General principles	91
6.2	Controlled writing by combining	91
6.2.1	Combining by matching	91
6.2.2	Combining by re-ordering	92
6.2.3	Combining using plans and outlines	93
6.3	Controlled writing by substitution	93
6.3.1	Substitution of words and phrases in sentences	94
6.3.2	Substitution of sentences in paragraphs using plans and outlines	96
6.3.3	Substitution of paragraphs in longer pieces using plans and outlines	99

7 Guided writing 102

7.1	General principles	102
7.2	Guided writing by completion	102
7.2.1	Completion by matching	103
7.2.2	Completion by multiple choice questions	103
7.2.3	Completion using plans and outlines	103
7.3	Guided writing by reproduction	104
7.3.1	Reproduction by matching	104
7.3.2	Reproduction by multiple choice questions	105
7.3.3	Reproduction by copying	105
7.4	Guided writing by compression	105
7.4.1	Compression by underlining	105
7.4.2	Compression using plans and outlines	106
7.5	Guided writing by paraphrase	106
7.5.1	Paraphrase by matching	107
7.5.2	Paraphrase by comparing	107
7.5.3	Paraphrase by multiple choice questions	108
7.5.4	Paraphrase by copying	109

8   **Free writing**   110

8.1   General principles   110
8.2   Free writing by expansion   112
8.3   Free writing by completion   116
8.4   Free writing by translation   117
8.5   Free writing by transposition   118
8.6   Free writing using pictures   119
8.7   Free writing in games   121

Glossary   125
Bibliography   128
Index   135

Introduction

The purpose of this book is to apply contemporary language teaching principles to the teaching of writing. It provides essential information about the nature of writing skills and the kinds of exercises that can be used to teach them.

Part One outlines the overall approach to the teaching of written English, and the three chapters of Part Two deal with the skills that every writer needs. They will enable teachers to clarify their teaching aims.

Part Three is a collection of ideas for writing exercises. It sketches the principles underlying the preparation of exercise material, and illustrates them with a large number of exercise types. It is a compendium, to be used as a source of ideas for teaching. But everything suggested in the four chapters of Part Three must be understood in the light of the approaches to teaching described earlier.

Since the focus of this book is on writing skills and useful exercises, the actual classroom management of writing lessons is not discussed in detail. There are many practical hints as well as lesson samples, but teachers will want to adapt the ideas given here to their own special needs in the many different teaching situations they encounter. Those who wish to read comments on the presentation of writing lessons should look at Byrne (1979) or White (1979).

The approaches and exercise types described in this and later chapters will be found in practice in the three books of the Macmillan Writing Series, edited and largely written by myself:

Writing in English 1 Anita Pincas, assisted by K Allen.

Writing in English 2 Anita Pincas, assisted by B Johnson and K Allen.

Writing in English 3 Anita Pincas, J Hadfield and C Hadfield.

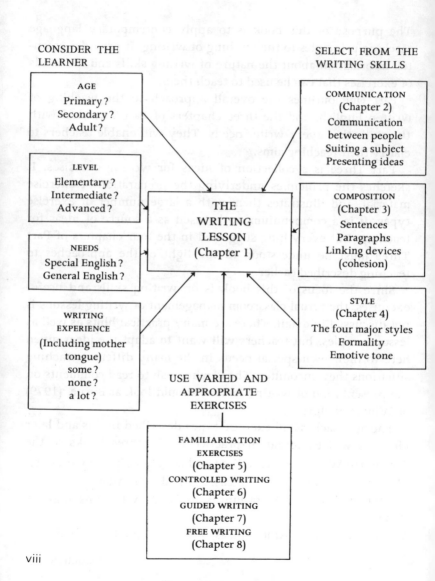

CONSIDER THE LEARNER

AGE
Primary?
Secondary?
Adult?

LEVEL
Elementary?
Intermediate?
Advanced?

NEEDS
Special English?
General English?

WRITING EXPERIENCE
(Including mother tongue)
some?
none?
a lot?

SELECT FROM THE WRITING SKILLS

COMMUNICATION
(Chapter 2)
Communication between people
Suiting a subject
Presenting ideas

COMPOSITION
(Chapter 3)
Sentences
Paragraphs
Linking devices (cohesion)

STYLE
(Chapter 4)
The four major styles
Formality
Emotive tone

THE WRITING LESSON
(Chapter 1)

USE VARIED AND APPROPRIATE EXERCISES

FAMILIARISATION EXERCISES
(Chapter 5)
CONTROLLED WRITING
(Chapter 6)
GUIDED WRITING
(Chapter 7)
FREE WRITING
(Chapter 8)

PART ONE
THE WRITING LESSON

1 Starting to prepare a writing lesson

1.1 Teaching aims

The teaching of writing should fulfil three main aims:

1 Its scope must be widened to go beyond the artificial, unrealistic school-type compositions of traditional teaching, to more genuine practical and relevant kinds of writing. The Chart opposite shows the enormous range of varieties of English writing that are used in the world today. Although some of them are very different from conventional essays, all are typical instances of useful written English. Students should practise as many varieties as possible.

2 The writing should be as communicative, or functional, as possible. That is, it should be seen to fulfil the sort of normal communicative purposes, or functions, that writing is used for in everyday life.

3 It should go beyond merely reinforcing grammar and vocabulary lessons and deal quite specifically with those skills that are required for effective writing. Every writing lesson should aim to teach one or two of the skills described in Chapters 2 to 4. Although written English should certainly support and be integrated with grammar and vocabulary learning, the teaching of writing should be recognised as a special part of language teaching, with its own aims and techniques.

Varieties of Written English

PERSONAL	PUBLIC	
	GENERAL	OCCUPATIONAL

PERSONAL	GENERAL	OCCUPATIONAL

Memory aids
a Lists
  -shopping
  -packing
  -jobs, etc
  -train times
  -reminders
b Personal
  -addresses
  -phone nos.
  -shop names
  -book names
  -birthdays, etc
c Notes
  -diaries
  -recipes, etc
Study aids
Lecture notes
Summaries
New vocabulary
Diary (journal)
Letters (personal)
Telegrams
Interpersonal
Invitations,
condolences,
thanks, birthday cards,
Christmas & Easter cards,
Valentines, etc
	Public signs
	Notices
	Posters
	Captions
	Recorded information
	Eye-witness
	accounts, etc
	Instructions and Messages
	a Receiver not
	  present
	  -with products
	  -to family,
	  employees,
	  others
	b Receiver present
	  -in library
	  -lecture
	  -game (eg treasure
	  hunt)
	Entertainment
	Word puzzles, skits,
	songs, cartoon jokes,
	games, etc
	Speeches
	Drama
	Theatre, opera, film
	(Auto)biography
	Fiction (including
	comics)
	Poetry and Songs
	Menus
		Classification
		Book indexes, record-
		keeping, dictionaries,
		recipes, catalogues, etc
		Committee Minutes
		Advertisements
		Form-filling
		Passport, social
		security, customs,
		identity, cheques,
		insurance, bills,
		house sales, bank,
		Computer dating, etc
		Applications
		Letters, & character
		references
		Letters (non-personal):
		Orders, inquiries, sale,
		complaints, appeals, etc
		Debates
		Speeches
		Conventions, public
		meetings, interviews, etc
		Notice Board items
		(personal)
		Public Information
		a Tourist
		b Banking
		c Transport
		d Journalism
		  -sport
		  -headlines
		  -weather
		  -news
		  -science, etc
		e Government
		  -statutes
		  -regulations, etc
			Specifications
			Engineering plans,
			computer programmes,
			patent applications, etc
			Educational
			All subjects
			  -textbooks, essays,
			  -reports, manuals,
			  -handbooks,
			  - encyclopaedias
			Note-taking
			By doctor, police,
			estate agent,
			dentist, etc
			Legal
			Contracts, law reports,
			commentaries, instructions,
			court presentations
			Commercial
			Letters, reports,
			records, announcements,
			committee minutes,
			surveys, stock lists,
			inventories, bills,
			receipts, etc
			Questionnaires
			Market research, medical,
			census, etc
			Advertising
			Newspaper, radio, TV,
			poster, leaflets,
			brochures
			Journalism
			Interviews
			a Articles
			  -obituary
			  -political
			  -horoscopes, etc
			b Reviews
			  -theatre
			  -book
			  -records
			  -film
			  -concert, etc

A distinction has to be made between, on the one hand, an approach that sees writing as extended practice in the use of learned vocabulary and structures and, on the other hand, an approach that aims towards communicative competence in various forms of written English. The former leads to the familiar 'composition' of many classrooms. For instance, when the past tense forms have to be practised, past tense narrative is written; for future tense forms there are compositions about 'My future' or 'My next holiday'; for conditionals, the well-known 'What I would do if I won £1 million'. Such writing does have a legitimate role in language work. It gives practice, and it is useful for testing. But it is not motivated by a desire to teach writing as such. This book is concerned with the second, the communicative approach, which suggests that teaching material should be chosen for its intrinsic usefulness and interest. Selection must be influenced by the language level of the learners, but as far as possible the teacher should fit the structures to the writing and not *vice versa*.

Of course, the selection should be made in the light of the teacher's feelings about what is likely to best motivate his class. For instance, a common problem is to find elementary materials suitable for adults. Those designed for children will not interest older learners, for whom narrative skills probably have little importance. Their motivation will be greater with instructions, short advertisements, unadorned descriptions of products, simple letters, etc.

For all ages, and all levels, motivation is increased if writing is placed in a realistic context. Older students who are already literate in their own language will be able to draw on their knowledge of the functions of writing. But younger students of more limited experience need to realise that it is often important *to write rather than speak*, and further, to write *in English*. The best method is to demonstrate genuine pieces of written English and show how, where and why they are used. Teachers can collect samples of English from newspapers, tourist agencies, banks, government offices, personal correspondence and the other sources open to them. In addition, some of the books listed in Section 5 of the Bibliography on page 132 can provide useful materials. It is also very motivating to realise that the written exercises in the classroom can be used immediately in real letters to pen-friends, for instance, or to organisations like English by Radio (BBC), or the British Council.

Finally, a strong incentive can be provided by the use of group activities and games within the writing lesson. All three books in the *Writing in English* series referred to earlier make use of these methods. Writing does not have to be a lonely task. A small group of four or five students often enjoy cooperating to produce a set of instructions, a poster or an argument. And writing games can, of course, emphasise the importance of writing effectively and accurately to produce the results needed to win a game. For ideas about games see Chapter 8, and *How to Use Games in Language Teaching* (Rixon 1981).

1.2 Integrating writing into a course

In planning their work on written English, teachers usually have a choice of one of these three procedures:

1   They can devise their own writing scheme.

This first option would be every teacher's ideal: a special course that was tailor-made for every different group of learners (some would say for every different individual!). Most teachers, however, have neither the time nor the authority to devise their own syllabuses and programmes. Nor would many have the necessary expertise.

Devising a writing scheme would mean planning exactly what a group of learners needed to write, working out a progressive sequence of stages, collecting materials and exercises from numerous sources, and writing special exercises where none could be found ready-made. This is obviously a time-consuming and expert activity. Teachers who do feel that they can manage it will find that the description of writing skills in the next three chapters provides the essential content of such a writing course, while the last four chapters are a source from which they can draw exercise ideas.

2   They can use a published writing course and fit it in with the work from the text they happen to be using for their general language teaching.

This second option offers many convenient solutions to teaching problems. Two writing courses at present available, the *Macmillan Writing Series* (see page vii) and the three books by T C Jupp and J Milne, *Basic Writing Skills in English*, *Guided Paragraph Writing*, and *Guided Course in English Composition*, (see Bibliography: Section 2) both give a good selection of writing exercises, graded according to vocabulary and structure. The teacher's notes for all these workbooks indicate the language level of the different exercises and help determine how they can be dovetailed with a general language textbook. Teachers will have to include a few bridging exercises where the written work does not quite match the textbook.

For the teacher who chooses this option, this book should provide the basic understanding of the principles that lie behind ready-made writing courses, and practical help in devising the necessary bridging exercises between them and the class textbook.

3   They can use a variety of exercises, some from published books, some written by themselves, and fit these in with their work from the class text.

This third option is probably the one most commonly adopted

by teachers. Although virtually every coursebook for the teaching of English contains composition exercises, the function of these exercises is for the most part to consolidate the vocabulary and structures of the unit in which they are placed. There is no general language course that has a built-in writing course based on a principled approach to the teaching of writing skills. So, a teacher who wishes to take such a principled approach has to supplement his course with writing exercises of his own choice.

For the teacher who prefers this third option, then, the description of writing skills and writing exercises in the later chapters will provide a guide and source for the preparation of supplementary lessons. It should also help to avoid the dangers in option 3, namely that the supplementary written work becomes a rather random affair, slotted into the occasional slack period or obligatory homework, and dealing with whatever topics happen to have come up in the last lesson.

Instead of this, teachers can devise a special writing course to fit in the general language work (or to stand alone), as follows:

1 *either* *a* Choose some varieties of written English that would be meaningful and motivating for the class, and then

       b Observe what skills are needed for these varieties

or

       a Decide what writing skills will have to be taught, and then

       b Find meaningful and motivating varieties of written English that can be used to demonstrate and practice those skills.

(See the Chart of Varieties on page 3 and Chapters 2 to 4 on writing skills.)

2 Check on the language needed for those varieties (or, conversely, simplify the samples to fit the level of the learners).

3   Prepare suitable exercises to make a series of writing lessons based on each variety in turn (See section 1.1).

It is most useful to prepare a brief course outline. Such an outline might look like the one on pages 10 and 11, which is adapted from *Writing in English 2* (the second book in the Macmillan Writing Series, mentioned on page vii).

The importance of a course outline is that it helps the teacher to see how systematically he is covering the ground, indicates whether there is a good balance of material, enables lesson preparation well in advance, avoids repetition but suggests intervals for revision—in short, it gives the teacher a good overview of what he is doing, and a timetable against which he (and the students) can measure progress.

It is important to realise that there is no accepted grading of writing skills even in broad outline as there is of vocabulary and structure. The sample course was prepared for intermediate students, but it is the *language* column that determines this, not the varieties of English or the writing skills involved.

Some aspect of any of the writing skills can in fact be taught at any level. It is quite mistaken, for instance, to think that narrative is the only kind of writing suitable for elementary students. As the following examples show, combining simple sentences into short paragraphs to fulfil useful functions is the start of genuine written English, and can be done even with elementary level structures:

Expository writing with a definition:

> Mammals have warm blood. Young mammals get milk from their mothers. Humans are mammals.

Explanation:

> Milk is good for children. It has calcium for their bones.

Argument:

> Our country does not want nuclear power. It is dangerous and expensive. We do not need it.

Description (differences and similarities):

> Animals can walk but plants cannot. However, both animals and plants need air and water. They are living things.

Elementary level exercises tend to focus on short pieces, exemplifying one main skill at a time, and can be seen as building blocks ready to be grouped together and used for longer pieces. Many varieties of realistic writing, even if somewhat simplified, can and should be started at early levels.

Another fact to bear in mind when integrating writing exercises into a set language course is that many texts limit the written work at early level English to 'spoken English written down' (eg dialogues) rather than genuine 'written English'. It would be useful even at elementary level to start teaching the difference between spoken and written forms of English where the textbook does not do so. The difference includes contrasts between full forms and contractions, between short (perhaps 'incomplete') sentences and longer constructions, between informal and more formal vocabulary (eg *kid/child, mum/mother*). It is a sound idea to start by simply recording what has been, or could be, said. But inverted commas should be used to signal clearly that there is a distinction between speech written down and actual written English.

When writing exercises are done at elementary or intermediate levels, a limiting factor is always the small vocabulary of the students. It is therefore a good idea to teach the use of a dictionary as soon as possible. After all, finding a new word is much

COURSE OUTLINE

VARIETY	MATERIALS		WRITING SKILLS
1 Personal letter	Photos of blocks of flats	Describing and comparing	*Linking word both, the firs one, the seco one, but, however, on the other hand*
2 Tourist guide	Photos and map of Japan	Describing a country	*in addition besides, for example*
3 History	Pictures of Henry VIII and six wives	Narrative	*first, next, then, after that, finally*
4 Reports of real events	Diagram of street showing accident	Description and narrative	Revision of items from previous units

LANGUAGE	EXERCISE TYPES
Comparative adjectives	Filling in blanks
	Joining part-sentences
	Sorting out mixed-up sentences to make a paragraph
	Drawing and then describing a picture
Present simple	Matching pictures and paragraphs
Can	
There is/There are	Joining sentences with linking words
	Multiple choice of linking words
	Sorting out mixed sentences to make a paragraph
	Free writing
Simple past of irregular verbs	Filling in blanks (guided by pictures)
	Free writing (guided by pictures)
	Game: 'Consequences'
Past continuous tense vs. simple past	Filling in blanks (guided by pictures)
	Underlining linking words
	Joining part-sentences
	Using paragraph and story plan to re-order mixed-up sentences
	Free story-writing following a plan

easier than working out a new sentence structure, so the judicious use of a dictionary can open up writing possibilities in topic areas that the general English course does not cover.

Supplementary writing exercises may be based either on new material or on some of the materials in the course being used. Passages in the course text or in related readers will probably cover several varieties of written English and exemplify certain writing skills. They can be exploited for further exercises on writing. This is part of a longer passage on the dangers of smoking from *English for Adults* (W Blemiel, A Fitzpatrick, and J Quetz, Oxford University Press, Oxford, 1980). It is used in the text to practise *-ing* forms such as in 'the man living next door to me . . .' or 'seeing is believing'.

---

[1]Few people like changing their habits, good or bad, and, whether it is smoking, drinking or over-eating, they continue 'enjoying' them to the end, often the bitter end. [2]On every packet of cigarettes and in every advertisement, Americans are warned against the dangers of smoking: 'Warning: The Surgeon General Has Determined That Cigarette Smoking is Dangerous to Your Health'. [3]In spite of this, millions of them start smoking or go on smoking. [4]Why? [5]One reason may be that people watch their 'heroes' on TV drinking alcohol, smoking cigarettes and fighting their way from adventure to adventure, 'heroes' who seem to fear nothing, neither killing other people nor killing themselves—with alcohol and cigarettes. [6]If they are not afraid of the effects of smoking and drinking alcohol, why should John Smith, sitting at home in his armchair watching all this, be afraid?

The passage is in popular essay style, and can be used to teach paragraph construction. It follows the plan opposite.

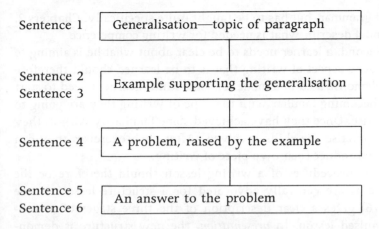

Sentence 1	Generalisation—topic of paragraph
Sentence 2 Sentence 3	Example supporting the generalisation
Sentence 4	A problem, raised by the example
Sentence 5 Sentence 6	An answer to the problem

Students then write more paragraphs using the same plan for different topics—the fact that warnings fail to prevent people from ruining their teeth with sugar, for example. To give more help, the teacher presents a frame using the key words of the model:

Few people like changing . . . .
Many magazines and television programmes . . . .
. . . . In spite of this . . . . Why?
One reason may be that . . . .

Thus, a passage in a general coursebook can illustrate a writing skill and lead to further exercises reinforcing that skill. With a little practice, teachers will be able to make considerable use of their course texts in this way. (For further discussion of paragraphs, see Chapter 3, Section 3.2.)

1.3 Teaching method

Two main principles underlie good teaching. First, writing competence does not follow automatically from adequate vocabulary and grammar, but has to be taught quite specifically. Chapters 2, 3 and 4 describe what is needed for writing competence.

Second, a learner needs to be clear about what he is aiming to do. Any aspect of writing that is to be learned should therefore be demonstrated in a model of some kind. Learners need to start by becoming familiar with the type of writing they are going to practise. Once they have achieved some familiarity with it, they can practise the skills involved. After such exercises they can try to produce their own piece of writing.

The procedures of a writing lesson should therefore be the same as are generally advocated for a structure lesson. Byrne (1976) gives a clear description of the three stages of a well-organised lesson. In *presentation*, the new structure is demonstrated so as to make its form and meaning clear. The teacher repeats it several times, either relating it to a picture, or miming an action, or in another simple way that illustrates its use. In *practice*, the class has an opportunity to get used to the new structure, repeating it after the teacher and gradually moving from pure drill to practice that allows some freedom. Finally, in *production*, the structure is made part of an activity where it has a genuine function. These three stages are not demarcated in the lesson; they merge into each other.

A writing lesson can fall into three similar stages: *familiarisation, controlled/guided exercises, free writing*. Chapters 5 to 8 deal with each of these in detail and suggest exercises for them. The following recommendations for lesson procedure give a brief illustration of the basic method.

1   FAMILIARISATION
Choose a writing skill or a variety of writing as the main point of the lesson, in the same way as you choose a structure as the objective of a language lesson. (See section 1.2) Then, demonstrate the target writing in an interesting and effective way.

Sometimes this can mean letting students read a passage of the kind they are going to write. But more often merely reading is not sufficient. Chapter 5 details a large number of exercises that help familiarisation. Three are illustrated here:

Sample 1

This exercise from *Writing in English 2* leads to close reading of a passage (the letter), and highlights its main features.

Steve is helping his Swedish friends who want to come and study in London.

> 104 Abbey Road,
> London SW 7.
> 18 August 1982
>
> Dear Gunnar and Ingrid,
>
> I'm trying very hard to find you a flat in London for your year's study here. It's difficult, but don't worry. I think I've found something.
>
> Yesterday I went to see two flats in Hammersmith. I think they are suitable because they are both near the hospital where you will study, but the first one is not in a good position. It's on a quiet street, but it's a long way from the underground station and from the nearest children's school. However, the flat itself is large and modern. It has big rooms, with nice furniture.
>
> The second one is on a very busy street. It's near the underground station and the school, but the building itself is old. The flat has medium-sized rooms, and only basic furniture. On the other hand, it's much cheaper than the first one: only £80 per week instead of £110.
>
> I asked the estate agent to wait for my answer, so please write quickly. Tell me which flat you prefer.
>
> Hoping to hear from you soon,
> Yours, Steve

Exercise 1 (i) This is a plan of Steve's letter. Use Steve's letter opposite to
Completion complete it.

Underlining (ii) Some important words in the plan are underlined. Find them in
Steve's letter and underline them there too.

The Flats	Good points		Bad points
both			
place	They are suitable because .... <u>both</u>		
	....		
the first one			
place	It's ....,	<u>but</u>	<u>it's</u> .... <u>and</u>
features	<u>However</u> .... <u>and</u> ..... <u>It</u>.........		
	....		
	<u>with</u>		
the second one			
place	.... <u>It's near</u>............		<u>is on</u>..............
features	`		<u>but</u> the building ..... The <u>flat</u> has......... <u>and</u> ....
cost	<u>On the other hand</u> ... . <u>the first one:</u>		
	....		

Sample 2
This exercise from *Writing in English 1* familiarises students with
logical order in description. An earlier exercise has presented a
model paragraph, in which the room is described clockwise
around a room-plan.

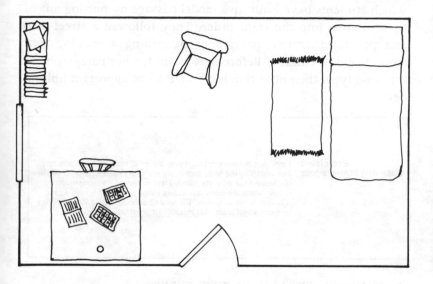

Choose the true sentences from the following list and use them to write a short paragraph about the second plan. Make the description go clockwise around the room.

1 There is a table and chair on the left of the door.
  There is a table and chair on the right of the door.

2 On the left, in one corner of the room, there is a small bookshelf.
  On the right, in one corner of the room, there is a small bookshelf.

3 Opposite the door there is a cupboard.
  Opposite the door there is an armchair.

4 My bed is by the wall opposite the window and in front of it there is a mat.
  My bed is by the wall opposite the door and in front of it there is a mat.

Sample 3

This is the last part of an exercise from *Writing in English 1* in which students have built up a model passage by putting mixed up sentences into the right order. They followed a street-map and put together two paragraphs describing a walking tour around central London. Before they write further paragraphs of the same type, their attention is directed to an important linking device.

Exercise 2 Look at your paragraphs. There are links between the sentences.
Observing linking words For instance, the same names are often in two sentences. Underline the second use of every name. Here is part of Paragraph 2:
  . . . There are many interesting shops in Oxford Street. Leave Oxford Street at Oxford Circus and continue along Regent Street to Piccadilly Circus. At Piccadilly Circus , . . .

---

2   CONTROLLED AND GUIDED EXERCISES

As in the practice stage of a language lesson, give students an opportunity to get used to the new writing skill by repeating it in controlled exercises, and then gradually move towards guided exercises that allow more freedom. (See Chapters 6 and 7: Controlled and guided writing). The difference between controlled and guided exercises is that in the former everything is presented so that students do little more than error-free (one hopes) copying, while in the latter they have choices, or can add something of their own and are thus likely to make mistakes.

In this stage of the lesson, the exercises move away from the material of the familiarisation work. The teacher's judgment in each case will determine just how much controlled or guided practice students need before proceeding to free writing. As a general rule give more rather than less!

The following two samples are from *Writing in English 3*.

Sample 1

This is a *controlled* exercise in a unit dealing with the presentation of generalisations and supporting facts.

Exercise 3
Rewriting

(1) Below is a table showing how people spend their evenings and a chart summarizing generalisations and facts taken from the table.

1 Use the information in the table to fill in the blanks in the *facts* column. Use language from the language summary.
2 Draw a line to match generalisations and facts.
3 Decide on an order for the sentences, to make them into a coherent paragraph.

Reading	3%
Sport	5%
Cinema	10%
Theatre	3%
Concert	2%
Listening to records	3%
Evening classes	2%
Clubs or societies	2%
Political meetings	1%
Hobbies (at home)	5%
Entertaining or social	15%
Restaurant	5%
Watching TV	44%

Generalisations	Facts
The survey also revealed that more people prefer ready-made entertainment to entertainment they provide for themselves.	Only .... of those questioned said they regularly practised a sport.
A new survey revealed that the majority of people spend their evenings at home rather than in social or sporting activities outside the home.	.... of those questioned said they spent their leisure time in such activities as watching TV, listening to records, reading or hobbies.
Finally, it would seem that, after a hard day's work people prefer not to engage in strenuous activity.	.... people said they spent their time watching TV or going to the theatre, cinema or concerts, while only .... people said they had a regular hobby.
For those who did go out in the evenings, social activities were more popular than cultural activities.	.... people spent their evening entertaining or dining out while only .... people regularly went to the theatre, concerts or cinema.

Sample 2

This *guided* exercise follows Sample 1 in the same unit.

Guided writing

(ii) These are the answers to a survey on people's reasons for working:

What is your main reason for working?	
	%
To pay the bills	10
Get rich	5
Provide for children	40
Buy a house	5
Get promotion	5
Enjoy my job	35

These generalisations can be made on the basis of the facts:

> The main motivating factors for most people to work, are personal satisfaction and family responsibilities.
>
> Ambition is not the main motivation for most people in their work.
>
> Surprisingly, money did not seem to play an important part in motivating people to work.

Add the supporting facts to each generalisation and join them together to form a paragraph. Add an introductory and a concluding sentence.

3 FREE WRITING

As in the production stage of a structure lesson, use the writing skill as part of a genuine activity such as a letter, story or essay. Writing games are also effective at this stage. The writing skill that has been practised in earlier exercises can now be used without the support that was previously given. There should be a link with the earlier work, but students should feel as if they are creating something of their own.

Sample

This is an example of a very simple free writing game from *Writing in English 1*. In the earlier exercises of the unit, students have practised describing character as revealed by handwriting.

Each student writes a sentence of eight to ten words on a piece of paper. He must not tell anyone his sentence but he must remember it. All the students then put their pieces of paper on a table and mix them up. Each student now takes one and writes a description of the handwriting and the writer underneath it. Then he puts the paper back on the table.

When everybody is finished, students find their own sentence and read the description.

Does your handwriting reveal your true personality?

Either at the end of the whole lesson, or at convenient times in the course of it, the teacher will have to correct his students' work. If the writing practice has been chosen to fit the language level of the class and the main structures were prepared or revised in advance, then correction will not be as much of a headache as in totally 'free' composition. With controlled exercises, where every student should produce the same thing, it is quite straightforward and students could correct their own or each other's work. A systematic teaching method is sure to reduce the number of errors, but in any case a communicative approach to writing requires a somewhat more tolerant attitude to them. In traditional composition, students are expected to demonstrate that they have mastered certain structures or vocabulary and the teacher will be looking for mistakes. But if the aim is to achieve a reasonable communicative competence, then the teacher will be more interested in whether the student has managed to put together a piece of writing that could fulfil a broad communicative function, eg a reasonably set-out letter, a logically organised description, a set of coherent instructions, and so on. It makes more sense in a *writing* lesson to correct only those errors that relate directly to the main aims of the lesson and to note others for revision at another time.

The three lesson stages provide a systematic and effective basis for a writing lesson. But 'lesson' need not be interpreted as 'one lesson period'. It could be spread over two or more periods, possibly including homework.

Moreover, to avoid boredom the order of the stages can be varied occasionally. For instance, free writing might sometimes be done first in order to help establish what skills the students lacked. In this case, the free writing would suggest controlled and guided exercises that would lead up to a second attempt at free writing of the same kind.

Furthermore, familiarisation is sometimes unnecessary when students are asked to write in a style they have already used on frequent occasions. A knowledge of their writing skills in the mother tongue can also be very helpful here.

In this outline of the teaching method, it was assumed that a writing lesson focussed on one writing skill at a time. But the teacher can use his judgment to decide when to teach more than one and, most important, when to bring several skills together in revision. Revision is an aspect of teaching that will be very much helped by the preparation of a course outline as suggested in the preceding section.

Although an intelligent flexibility is the heart of all sound teaching, the one general principle that should always be adhered to is that writing has to be *taught*. It does not grow inevitably out of extensive reading and free writing.

To summarise, the teaching method that has been outlined in this chapter can be briefly characterised as 'assisted imitation'. A guiding principle in the teaching of writing has always been the use of good models to emulate. Famous writers of the past as well as the present advise young authors to read widely and become acquainted with the best literature. This advice is even more relevant to foreign language learners who lack any acquaintance with written English. For them we require not only suitable models that they can imitate, but above all a system which provides the kind of detailed assistance they need. The lesson procedure suggested here, together with the rest of the ideas in this book, should provide the basis for such a system.

PART TWO
WRITING SKILLS

Introduction

Over and above the ability to write correctly and choose appropriate words, a writer needs some competence in each of the following nine areas. These are the essential writing skills from which a teacher can choose points for specific lessons.

1	Communication between people	
2	Suiting a specific subject	COMMUNICATION
3	Presenting ideas	
4	Constructing sentences	
5	Using paragraphs	COMPOSITION
6	Using linking devices (cohesion)	
7	Writing in the four major styles: narrative, descriptive, expository, argumentative	
8	Achieving the desired degree of formality	STYLE
9	Creating the desired emotive tone	

Every time a writer sets pen to paper he in fact makes choices about what he wants to do in each of these nine areas, and adjusts his language accordingly. But for teaching purposes it is more effective to isolate separate examples of such skills and gradually work towards integrating them into an overall writing competence.

Some teachers may wish to give priority to one or several of these skills. For instance, many students do not need to become competent in any other than a moderately formal style, just as many would not need to handle a wide range of emotive effects. Stylistic skills might then be given less attention than composition and communication skills. Again, some students may have had considerable practice in using paragraphs in their own language. So, for them, writing practice might emphasise, say, the use of linking devices or some aspects of the communicative skills.

As was pointed out in Chapter 1, Section 1.2, page 8, the skills themselves are not really gradable. It is the language that has to be adjusted to the students' level of English. If subject-matter is chosen so as to keep to an appropriate vocabulary level and to avoid complexities that students might not have the structures to deal with, then any of the writing skills can be taught at any level.

2   Communication

2.1 Communication between people

Writing is an integral part of everyday life. The Chart of Varieties of Written English on page 3 gives some indication of the vast range of activities for which it is used: from writing for oneself, where there are few conventions of style, through public and personal information, where there are some conventions, to largely impersonal written communication where there are fairly strict formalities to be observed.

The first step in teaching writing is therefore to select and demonstrate relevant varieties. English newspapers, magazines, imported products with English writing on the package, instructions, brochures from travel agents, banks or government delegations—all these can be brought into the classroom to add a touch of reality to uses of English.

The second step is to help students visualise how a piece of writing establishes communication between people, ie has a specific communicative function. What that function is in any particular case will depend on the writer's aim. He may want to report, evaluate, complain, advise, suggest, question, command, invite, etc. There is in fact an infinite number of such aims, given the diversity of human motives and needs. But most of the varieties on the Chart on page 3 have a number of common ones associated with them.

Business letters, for instance, very frequently make requests, agree or disagree with requests from others, give reminders, express urgency, offer to help, apologise, make suggestions, confirm, express dissatisfaction, etc. On the other hand, scientific texts usually describe observations, exemplify, make predictions, and so on. In contrast, the aim of advertising is largely to persuade, while that of committee minutes is solely to report, and the aim of letters of application for a job is to provide information in a favourable light.

Further ideas can be found in books which aim to teach communicative English. They often have the term 'functional' in the title. Although most of them deal with spoken English, they are very useful as source-material for written English as well. For instance *Feelings* (Duff and Jones 1980) deals with ways of expressing desire/longing, excitement/anticipation, worry/apprehension, admiration, irritation/impatience, delight/relief, indignation/annoyance, surprise, disappointment/regret, interest/-curiosity, uncertainty, sympathy/lack of sympathy. The terms 'notion' and 'notional' are also used rather loosely in some books to mean something very similar to 'communicative' or 'functional', and often indicate useful material. For instance J A van Ek, (1976) has useful lists of 'functions' and 'notions' together with related structures and vocabulary.

To develop his own ideas, the teacher can simply choose a variety of writing and then ask himself:

1 Who would be likely to write this? To whom?
2 Why? For what purpose?
3 In what circumstances?
4 Would s/he talk to anybody about it first?
5 Would the writing receive a reply?
6 If not, would there be any other consequence resulting from the writing?

The answers to such questions will give enough background

to set the writing in a realistic context and thereby help the students to understand its purpose.

The next step is to devise a method of helping students to fulfil a purpose adequately. The main technique, as described in Chapter 1, Section 1.3, is to show examples of the kind of writing that has to be produced and build exercises on them. But in addition students must develop an ability to visualise a reader and predict what he will be taking for granted and what he needs to be specifically told. They can be helped by class discussion and imaginative preparation on the teacher's part. But nothing is as effective as having a real reader to write for. So there should be frequent attempts to find real readers other than the teacher.

The problem can often be largely solved by group work and writing games which involve students in combined activities where they feel that their fellow-students will read what they write. This can add relevance and motivation to the task. For further comments on group work and games see Chapter 1, Teaching aims, page 5. Many of the useful ideas in *Teaching Techniques for Communicative English* (Revell 1981) can be adapted to the teaching of writing.

To summarise, communication between people takes many forms in writing, and all of them are part of 'written English'. Writing lessons should go beyond school essays to useful, practical varieties of English.

2.1.1 Classroom application

The following is a very simple example of how students can write for each other. It comes at the end of a unit in *Writing in English 1* that has practised letters of request and replies to them.

Exercise 4
Guided writing
Group activity

Each student writes a letter to an uncle, a grandmother, a teacher, the Prime Minister, etc, asking for something. For example, the letter to an uncle can ask for money, the letter to the grandmother can ask to borrow her best necklace, etc. The letter must ask for something special. The letter should use *because* and explain the reason why the writer is asking for something, eg 'I need ten pounds because I want to buy .... It costs .... pounds, and I have only .... pounds.'

The students do not sign with their own name. They use a false name. All the letters are then mixed up on a table, and each student takes one (not his own). They do not know whose letter they have taken.

Students now write a reply to the letter, saying either 'Yes', or 'No' and giving a reason, eg: 'Yes, I will gladly lend you ten pounds because you are a hardworking boy. I know you will not waste the money', or: 'No, I am sorry I cannot lend you ten pounds because I am afraid you will waste it. I know that you have wasted your own money.'

Everyone now finds his own letter and the reply, to discover if he can get what he asked for.

As well as writing for each other, students can join into small groups and plan their writing together. The procedure would be: First, they discuss in general what to write. Second, they compose sentences aloud, and improve on each other's suggestions until they are all satisfied. Then, they either appoint one person to write a clean copy or they each write their own copy.

The next sample shows students writing letters prepared by a small group. This activity comes at the end of a unit in *Writing in English 2* which used letters from 'agony' columns of magazines to practise asking for and giving advice.

Exercise 5
Writing game

Form small groups in the class and make a list of problems.
Working as a group, write a letter asking Helpful for advice about one of them.
Exchange letters with another group, and, still working as a group, write the reply.

Another kind of group activity is illustrated in the following exercise from a unit of *Writing in English 1* that has dealt with the London Marathon and practised writing instructions following a route-map.

Finally, the following is a simple writing game, known as 'Kim's game'. Students have practised describing spatial arrangements in preceding exercises. It is from *Writing in English 1*.

Further ideas are in Part Three.

2.2 Suiting a specific subject

The preceding section of this chapter dealt with communication between people. This section explains how the choice of subject-matter influences communication.

Most teachers, when preparing their class for writing about a certain subject, try to provide the necessary vocabulary and structures. This is adequate for writing of the traditional school essay type. But if teaching is to go beyond that to real-life varieties of written English, then it will not do. For instance, 'Why I like tennis', which at first sight is on a sporting subject, is still merely a topic for a school essay. Most writing about sport in the world outside the classroom is either reporting of events (in newspapers or magazines) or instructions for play (in handbooks or manuals). Genuine writing in the subject area of sport is therefore likely to be one of these two varieties. Each demands different kinds of communicative writing. Reporting events is a different type of communication and involves different skills from those needed to give instructions.

Any subject is closely bound up with a small set of varieties of writing and thus with the communicative aims of those varieties. To give further examples, writing in the area of science is likely to be of the textbook or academic journal variety, writing in the area of business is likely to involve correspondence, reports, minutes of committee meetings and forms, while writing about the theatre would probably be critical review or historical description. These links between subject and variety are matters of likelihood, not necessity. But for practical purposes, the teaching of writing should follow the most usual examples that occur.

A communicative approach to subject-matter, therefore, emphasises the need to prepare students not only with appropriate grammar and vocabulary, but also to fulfil the communicative aims normally associated with the subject area in question.

2.2.1 Classroom application

All writing should be seen to have a genuine purpose, and this can often be achieved if the writing is part of a larger project which is to be put together for school or college needs in other subjects, or for some genuine activity like publicising the activities of the school or club, or as part of a hobby the students enjoy pursuing. A hobby like stamp collecting or photography can lead to a project covering many different aspects of the subject, eg some history, some letters to associations and other interested hobbyists, some classification, some technical description, and so forth. The research effort involved in collecting information can be exploited along a number of different lines.

The sample exercise that follows is adapted from B J Thomas, *Practical Information* (1977). It shows how students (in this case advanced) can practise different kinds of writing related to one subject. They will write some description and instructions, and also devise a brochure of their own following the model given.

The Wellington Museum

Apsley House, Hyde Park Corner, W1V 9FA
Telephone 01-499 5676

Administered by the
Victoria and Albert Museum

Apsley House was presented to the Nation by the seventh Duke of Wellington in 1947, together with its contents. The exhibits include famous paintings, silver, porcelain, orders and decorations, and personal relics of the first Duke (1769–1852); also Canova's great marble figure of Napoleon Bonaparte. Apsley House was designed by Robert Adam for Lord Bathurst, and built 1771–78. It was bought by the Duke of Wellington in 1817, who employed Benjamin Wyatt to enlarge it, face it with Bath stone, and add the Corinthian portico (1828–29). The House was opened to the public as the Wellington Museum in the summer of 1952, and is administered by the Victoria and Albert Museum. An illustrated guide is on sale in the House.

TRANSPORT Bus or Underground (Piccadilly line) to Hyde Park Corner.

ADMISSION 10p Children under 16: 5p Old Age Pensioners: 5p Children under 12 must be accompanied by an adult, it is regretted that no reduction in admission fees can be made for parties, but under certain conditions organised parties of schoolchildren may be admitted free of charge. Enquiries about these conditions should be addressed to the Resident Officer.

HOURS OF OPENING
Every weekday including Saturdays and Bank Holidays: 10 a.m.–6 p.m.
Sundays: 2.30 p.m.–6 p.m.
Closed Good Friday, Christmas Eve, Christmas Day and Boxing Day.

Most of the museums and art galleries of Britain are free and many of them have free lectures, special exhibitions, bookshops and restaurants. The Duke of Wellington is one of Britain's most famous military heroes and is especially remembered for his defeat of Napoleon at Waterloo in 1815.

Composition

1 (O/W) You are a teacher and you are going to take your class on a visit to the Wellington Museum. Tell the class what the museum is and what they will see, how and when to get there to meet you, and any other details you think are necessary.

2 (W) Write a conversation between a friend and yourself. Your friend wants to know about the Wellington Museum, what there is to see there and how much it costs to get in. Write in dialogue form, giving only the name of each speaker, followed by his or her words.

3 (W) Imagine that in 150 years from now the house where you now live in your country is famous because you became a famous person. Following the arrangement on the opposite page and making the same divisions into history, transport, admission and hours of opening, write a similar leaflet (the same length or shorter) for 'The (your name) Museum'.

2.3 Presenting ideas

The earlier sections of this chapter discussed writing as communication between people and how this related to the choice of subject. This section adds another important skill to the list of those needed for effective communication—the clear presentation of ideas.

There is a certain logic involved—probably universal—in the way we present our ideas. We refer to different kinds of presentation with expressions like classification, description of processes, hypothesis, giving reasons, describing similarities, etc. These are often called 'functions' or 'notions' by other writers. We shall refer to them as 'logical functions'.

The following is a short list of some of the major logical functions that a writer must learn to express. Each is listed together with a question that a teacher could use in class to bring out the essentials of that function. There are also some topics that would probably require it, and a sample sentence and paragraph to show just two of the many ways it can be expressed in English. Any logical function can constitute the teaching aim of a lesson procedure as described in Chapter 1.

Presentation of ideas is discussed again in Chapter 3, Sections 3.1 and 3.2, in relation to sentence and paragraph construction.

LOGICAL FUNCTIONS

1 DESCRIPTION OF FEATURES

a Definition What is it? *Topics:* Houses, Democracy, Courage, Love, Nationalism, A Ruler, A Bicycle Pump, A Thermometer, An Abacus, A Compass, A Motor.

> *Sample sentence:* A house is a building that people live in.
>
> *Sample paragraph:* A star is a kind of giant nuclear reactor, producing heat and light. In this way it differs from the Moon or a planet such as Venus, which do not produce

light but merely reflect that of the Sun. Another difference is that while the Moon and the planets are solid, a star is so hot that all the chemical elements of which it is made are in the form of gas.

(from T R Entwhistle and J Cooke, eds, *The Junior General Knowledge Encyclopaedia*, Octopus Books, London 1978)

b *Classification* What kinds are there? *Topics:* Means of transport, Sports and pastimes, Climate and weather conditions, Military organisations, Housing, The animal kingdom, Useful inventions, Trades and professions, Types of Art, Plants.

Sample sentence: There are three main kinds of transport: land, sea and air.

Sample paragraph: The world contains many forms of energy, but all of them come from two sources only—the sun and minerals. The sun's energy reaches the earth in the form of light and heat; minerals give us energy in chemical form.

c *Description* What does it look/sound/feel/smell/taste like? *Topics:* My home; My favourite city, A country I have visited, A jumbo-jet, A novel, Sugar, Tourists, A lovely building/tree/person, My most treasured possession, Myself at present/in the past/in ten years' time, Spring, An important man.

Sample sentence: My home is small in size, but it contains everything I need.

Sample paragraph: My room is small and comfortable. My bed is against the wall opposite the door, and there is a mat in front of the bed. On the right, there is a small bookshelf in the far corner of the room, and an armchair in the near corner. To the left of the door, under the window, there is a table and a chair. My pictures are on the wall opposite the window.

2 DESCRIPTION AND/OR EXPLANATION OF A PROCESS

How does it work? *Topics:* Obtaining a passport and visa for travel; Changing a tyre; Mending a fuse; Cooking a dish; Arranging a party; Parliament creating a new law; How something works, eg a telescope, a microscope, a submarine, a lighthouse, a fountain pen, a ball-point pen, a telephone, radar; How social processes work, eg marriage ceremony, initiation ceremony, religious ceremony, committee meeting, club activities, picnics; How natural processes work, eg the weather, plant respiration, crop growing, evolution.

Sample sentence: Things can be pushed by the steam from boiling water.

Sample paragraph:

How bread is made

Bread consists of four main ingredients: flour, salt, yeast and water. To begin with, these ingredients are weighed. Then they are mixed together in a mixer to produce dough. The dough is cut into large pieces, and these are rolled in a rolling machine. Next, the rolled dough is cut and weighed into one pound pieces. These pieces of dough are then rolled in another roller, after which the rolled pieces are shaped before being placed in baking tins. After this, the filled tins are put into large, hot ovens where the loaves are baked for between twenty and thirty minutes. When the hot loaves come out of the ovens, they are cooled, and then they are sliced (if necessary), after which the sliced loaves are wrapped. Finally, the wrapped loaves are packed and then they are distributed to shops to be sold.

(from R V White, *Functional English 2 Exploitation*, Nelson, 1979, page 46.)

---

3 SEQUENCE OF EVENTS

What comes next? What came before? *Topics:* The history of

something, eg jazz, a country; a football club, medicine; Personal history, eg Memories of childhood, How a friend was made, Waiting for an important letter (or phone-call, etc), An adventure (real or imaginary), A meal in a restaurant, A visit to a doctor or dentist, etc, A frightening experience; general narrative, eg Recent changes in fashion (clothing, music, food, housing); An old man and a child alone in a house; A strange invention and its effects on the community; The life of an only child; The story of a novel, or film, or TV programme.

Sample sentence: He always gets up when the alarm clock rings at 8am.

Sample paragraph: See Section 3.3.1, second sample exercise.

4 CAUSE-EFFECT OR EFFECT-CAUSE
What causes it? What does it cause? *Topics:* Way of living and health; New technology; Unjust laws; Over-crowding in cities; The different social roles of men and women; Friendships; Violence and war; A natural disaster, eg a volcano, an earthquake; The popularity of something or someone, eg a hairstyle, an actor or singer; Cheating in exams; Hijacking of aeroplanes; Ambition; Jealousy.

Sample sentence: See Section 2.3.1 sample exercise.

Sample paragraph: Human error gives rise to many road accidents. For instance, drinking alcohol causes drivers to be less alert. They often fail to notice other cars or pedestrians. But even alert drivers can misjudge distance and speed. Accidents often result from such errors.

5 REASONS FOR ACTIVITIES OR STATES OF AFFAIRS
Why? *Topics:* I like jazz; Why I have bought a motorbike; Flying is spoiling travel; I lost my temper; It is right to do body transplants; Life begins at forty; Sweets should be banned; Capital punishment is necessary; Why I would like to be a . . . (eg doctor, teacher, builder); Why I would not like to be . . . (eg President of the US, head of a large family).

Sample sentence: I like my summer holidays because I can go swimming.

Sample paragraph: Some people like to paint furniture or the rooms in their house, but I do not enjoy it. It takes a long time to get the paint mixed. It is hard to apply the paint evenly; it always seems to streak. The paint gets on my clothes, my arms, and sometimes my face. I also drop it from the brush and have to wipe it from places where it is not supposed to be.

(Horn 1977)

6 SIMILARITIES

What features do they have in common? *Topics:* Two sports; Two friends; Christianity and Islam; Foods in Asia; Ancient and modern superstitions; Different languages; A nation is a large family; Life is a game of football; How birds build nests.

Sample sentence: My cat and dog are both very friendly.

Sample paragraph:

Modern college students, driving to classes in modified sports cars and living somewhat modified scholarly lives, may not feel any special kinship with the medieval students of Oxford and Cambridge. But, regardless of the separation of time and space, students have always been concerned about their privileges and their finances. Today, student rights is a lively issue on many college campuses, and much publicized demonstrations are supposed to be typical of our unsettled modern times. But medieval students also dissented on many issues, and the famous 'town and gown' riots in England were much bloodier and more violent than student protests today. The subject of free speech was as much an issue in the thirteenth century as it is in the twentieth. But the greatest similarity between past and present student life is the perennial battle of the budget. Today, students pull in their belts as they watch expenses gobble up their small incomes or allowances. Yet, back in 1220, we find a student writing to his father that although he was 'studying with the greatest diligence . . . you know that without clothes and food and wine your son grows cold.'

7 CONTRASTS

How are they different? *Topics:* Flying *vs* train travel or sailing; Punishment and reward; Two ways to lose weight; Two jobs you have had (or would like); The same subject taught in school and college; Life on a farm and in a city; Two teachers; Several family members; Customs of different countries; Two Nobel Prize winners.

Sample sentence: Whereas the city is crowded and dirty, the country is empty and clean.

Sample paragraph: In answer to your enquiries about cheap fares from London to Paris, here are two possible methods of travel.

You can go by a combination of coach, ferry, and train. The ferry crosses the Channel from Dover to Calais, where you can get a train to Paris. The trip one way, from London to Paris, takes a bit more than ten hours, and a ticket costs forty pounds. However, if you choose this way of travelling, you'll have to travel either on Friday or on Sunday. Alternatively, you may want to go all the way by coach. The coach leaves from Victoria Station to Paris, takes fourteen hours, and a ticket costs twenty-five pounds. If you choose a coach trip, you'll be able to travel either on Thursday, Friday or Sunday.

8 GENERALISATIONS AND RELATED FACTS

What further facts are there? *Topics:* Punctuality; Cleanliness; Astrology; Gravity; Inflation; Vaccination; Racialism; Strike while the iron is hot; A stitch in time saves nine; Better late than never; Why (or why not) you are similar to others of your own age; Concern for the environment; 'My country, right or wrong'; TV influences people's lives; What is luck?; Humour; Politics; Strangers.

Sample sentence: Disagreements between parents and children show that they see the world differently.

Sample paragraph: Twenty-five years ago many families were satisfied with a home that had only one electric socket. Such a house would also commonly have had no hot water supply. The electric wiring would not have been designed to accept any load greater than a single-bar heater. Indeed, older houses had electric lighting downstairs only. Living standards have risen: what were once considered to be reasonably comfortable homes are now unacceptable for even the poorest families. These improved standards have increased the demand for electricity.

(from M J Wallace, *Study Skills in English*, Cambridge University Press, Cambridge, 1980: page 89.)

9 HYPOTHESES AND ARGUMENTS FOR THEM

Why do you think this is likely to be true? *Topics:* Men and women will always be different; Music appeals to the emotions; The continents of the earth are moving; In a murder mystery (eg from a given story), the murder must have been . . . ; There is no way of measuring intelligence; There must be other intelligent beings in the universe; English is becoming the world language; Money is the root of evil.

Sample sentence: Astronomers have made tests which suggest that the universe is expanding.

Sample paragraph:

One theory is that cultivation of the grape originated in the area around the Caspian Sea. From there grape growing spread to neighbouring areas of Asia Minor, then to Greece, and from Greece to Sicily. The Phoenicians took the grape into France, and the Romans planted grapes in Germany and England. At the same time as grape cultivation spread into the West, grapes were carried into the East by way of India. Everywhere that new lands were settled, people took the grape along. Columbus and later colonists brought the European grape to America, where it had little success until it was crossed with the native American varieties.

(Imhoof and Hudson 1975: page 67.)

10 FOR AND AGAINST
What are the issues on both sides of the argument? *Topics:* Tradition; Censorship; Divorce; Nuclear power; Space travel; Various types of education; Smoking in public places; Advertising; Royalty; Cutting down forests; Saving rare animals; Compulsory military training for boys and girls; Should I choose . . . ? (eg a certain profession, a type of car, a particular spouse, a new hairstyle, etc).

> *Sample sentences:* Although nuclear energy has its risks, it is needed for technological development.
>
> *Sample paragraph:* There are two sides to the argument about censorship. On the one hand, most people desire liberty to think, speak and write as they please. But on the other hand, no one likes to see dangerous or immoral viewpoints being presented in ways that would corrupt young people.

Further ideas are in Part Three.

2.3.1 Classroom Application

Overleaf is part of an exercise from J Moore, *Concepts in Use*, 1980. (Note that 'concept' is another term often used to mean virtually the same as 'logical function'.) It aims to show how the cause-effect relationship can be expressed. The book is intended for beginners of English with a special interest in the language of science, but cause-effect relations are also very common in general English.

Activity 1

Read the following statements and identify the cause and the effect in each statement. For example,

Cause   Effect

Malaria	can result in	chronic ill health.

1 Many industrial accidents are due to carelessness.
2 Polluted water supplies lead to epidemics.
3 A high fever brings about dehydration.
4 Human error is the cause of most road accidents.
5 Accidents in factories often result from ignorance of safety regulations.
6 Exposure to traffic fumes may result in lead poisoning.
7 The use of electrical equipment by unqualified persons may give rise to fatal accidents.

Activity 2

1 Match each cause with a corresponding effect.
One has been done for you.

	CAUSE		EFFECT
i	air pollution	a	mental and physical ill heal
ii	deficiency of vitamin D	b	anaemia
iii	lack of hygiene	c	family and financial problem
iv	deficiency of iron	d	cholera and typhoid
v	alcoholism	e	inadequate bone growth
vi	dependence on drugs	f	diseases of insanitation
vii	micro-organisms called pathogens	g	pulmonary diseases

2 Now write a statement about each cause.

Further ideas are in Part Three.

3 Composition

3.1 Sentences

In order to convey thoughts and feelings as clearly as possible we do several things. We arrange our ideas in sentences, we organise sentences into paragraphs, and with these we construct whole essays, stories, etc. We use special words, phrases, and other devices to indicate just how the ideas, sentences and paragraphs actually relate to each other. The result is a stretch of language that we have composed—a composition.

Most commonly, composition is discussed in relation to paragraph building and essay planning. In fact, however, it starts at sentence level. The very simplest way of expressing an idea is in one bare sentence, eg 'I have a ball'. If further ideas, or information, are to be added then we could do so with more of such bare sentences, eg 'The ball is big', 'The ball is green', etc. But we do not normally express ourselves in a succession of such simple statements. We put the various pieces of information together in any of a large number of different ways, eg 'I have a big green ball' or 'I have a ball that is big and green' or 'My ball is a big green ball' or 'The big green ball is mine' or 'My big ball is green', etc.

Teachers are often puzzled by the way students who can handle fairly complex sentences in grammar exercises, nevertheless do not use them but slip back into a series of bare sentences when writing a composition. The reason is that grammar work alone does not provide practice in *making use* of more complex sentences.

Very often, having practised a structure quite thoroughly, the teacher asks his students to write a composition using it. But he has not given them the *ability* to do so. This can be best acquired through a systematic teaching procedure which *demonstrates how* sentences are used in real pieces of written English and then *leads* students to write them in controlled and guided exercises. Only after such specific teaching are students likely to feel confident and able to apply their structure learning to actual writing tasks.

The most useful procedure is to choose a writing skill and then isolate the elements needed for it. For instance, description of spatial arrangements can start from a list of key items related to a familiar place, eg the school. Students are given a list of the key items in very simple sentences:

There is a kitchen.

The kitchen is at the back of the school.

The kitchen is on the left.

There are two toilets.

The toilets are to the right of the kitchen.

There is a classroom.

The classroom is in the front of the school.

The classroom is on the right.

The classroom is the infants' classroom.

The infants' classroom has very low chairs.

The infants' classroom has very low tables.

The infants' classroom has many toys.

etc.

They are then shown how to combine these items of information in longer, more complex sentences. Finally, the new sentences can be arranged as a paragraph. Two possible paragraphs from the above would be:

1 There is a kitchen in the back left-hand corner of the school building, with two toilets to the right of it. Further along, in the front right-hand corner, is the infants' classroom which has very low chairs and tables and many toys.

2 In the back left-hand corner there is a kitchen. There are two toilets on the right, next to the kitchen. In the front right-hand corner of the building there is the infants' classroom. It has very low chairs and tables and many toys.

If necessary, a diagram can be given to help the description. Conversely, to make the exercise more difficult, the list of key items can be presented in a mixed-up order.

This kind of practice is more than merely sentence-combining. It is marshalling ideas and *using* sentences. The sample above is in elementary level English, but the very same principle should be applied at higher levels also.

3.1.1 Classroom application

Students need exercises in which they start from a number of separate facts and have to put these together in sentences. The facts can be given in charts, tables, diagrams, or in very simple, short sentences to be combined for effective writing.

The first sample overleaf is the last part of an exercise teaching students to organise contrasting ideas in short sentences. It is from Arnold and Harmer (1978).

In a recent survey, men and women of various ages were asked what they considered to be their main leisure activity. Here are the results.

Activities	Single men 15–30	Single women 15–30	Married men 20–30	Married women 20–30	Men 30–50	Women 30–50
Taking part in sport	17	15	10	5	6	2
Reading	7	10	8	10	4	10
Television	21	27	22	29	24	30
Drinking	16	5	20	3	25	5
Cinema	5	6	2	4	—	—
Watching sport	22	8	18	7	17	4
Gardening	1	3	5	5	10	7
Handicrafts	3	10	10	22	11	18
Studying	3	4		—	—	—
Dancing	4	10	1	5	—	7
Other activities	1	2	3	10	3	17
	100%	100%	100%	100%	100%	100%

Make contrasting generalisations about people's preferences as follows:

a Middle-aged men ... single men under 30
b Single women ... married women
c Single men ... married women
d Men ... women
e Single men under 30 ... married men under 30
f Young women ... middle-aged women
g Married men ... married women
h Gardening
i Studying
j Men taking part in sport ... men watching sport

The second sample is from *Writing in English 1*. Students have to combine simple facts related to pictures to create longer sentences suitable for a story.

Exercise 2
Joining sentences

Here are some more pictures for a story.

The fox and the bird (La Fontaine)

These sentences describe the pictures. Use them to write the story. Join the sentences with *and, but, so*. Omit the subject after *and* and *but*. When <u>the bird</u> is underlined, use *it* instead. When <u>the fox</u> is underlined, use *he*. You should have only six sentences in your story.

a A bird was hungry.
b <u>The bird</u> stole some cheese.
c <u>The bird</u> sat in a tree.
d The bird began to eat the cheese.
e The fox was hungry.
f The fox had no food.
g <u>The fox</u> praised the bird's voice.
h The fox asked <u>the bird</u> to sing.
i The bird was proud of its voice.
j The bird opened its mouth to sing.
k The cheese fell out of its mouth.
l The fox ran away with the food.

"You have a wonderful voice. Will you sing for me?"

Further ideas are in Part Three.

3.2 Paragraphs

It is perhaps easier to say, first, what a paragraph is not. It is not merely a succession of sentences neatly set out in the right shape:

> The trees are growing. He has been working for three hours now. I like yellow dresses. They are sending me a letter. It was summer there.

The next sample is not a paragraph either, even though there is an apparent theme to which all the sentences relate:

> The woman in the painting is smiling. He was an Italian painter. The Mona Lisa was painted by Leonardo da Vinci. There has been talk about the meaning of that smile for centuries. He lived during the Renaissance. People have different ideas about the meaning of the Mona Lisa's smile. They all agree that it is a great painting.

This is not a paragraph because there is no pattern in it. The sentences are jumbled rather like 'mat sat cat on the'. They can be arranged to make a paragraph, however:

> The Mona Lisa was painted by Leonardo da Vinci, an Italian painter who lived during the Renaissance. The woman in the painting is smiling and there has been talk about the meaning of her smile for centuries. People have different ideas about it. Nevertheless, all agree that the Mona Lisa is a great painting.

This arrangement makes an acceptable paragraph for two reasons:

1   It has a logical pattern. It is a descriptive paragraph, starting with historical information, then giving some detail about the nature of the topic, and concluding with an evaluative comment. This is fairly typical of the logic often used for the logical function of type 1c on page 37.

2   The sentences have been joined together or related to each other in certain ways:

a Some of the bare simple sentences have been joined to make one longer sentence (as was discussed in the previous section, 3.1).

b Links have been incorporated to relate the sentences to each other:

> *the painting* refers back to *The Mona Lisa*, *her* to *the woman*, *it* to *her smile*, *all* to *people*.
> *The Mona Lisa* is repeated in the last sentence.
> *Nevertheless* signals a contrast with the sentence before it.

The next section (3.3) describes such linking devices in more detail.

The first thing a writer has to do, then, is develop the skill of putting sentences together so as to create a paragraph that makes sense. In doing this, he can—indeed he must—assume that his reader is a logical person and will follow a logically arranged set of ideas. (There is some evidence that different cultures may follow different logical patterns, so a teacher should not dismiss a foreign student's work as illogical without considering this possibility.)

For each of the logical functions listed in Section 2.3, there are various fairly obvious ways of achieving a clear presentation of ideas within a paragraph. For instance, to describe an object one might move from one end to the other (eg a pencil), or from bottom to top (a tall building), or from outside to inside (a car). To describe a process it is most common to deal with each step in chronological order. An argument can move from generalisation to examples or *vice versa*. And so on.

The second thing a writer has to do is ensure that he provides enough signals (linking devices) for a reader to see how the sentences follow on from, support, or contrast with each other. When moving from one paragraph to the next, he will also use linking devices to show how each paragraph relates to the one preceding and the one following it. (See Section 3.3.)

In addition to these two considerations, writers make paragraphs easy to read by using one of the numerous common ways of opening and closing. They are listed here in no order of priority except for No 1 which is probably the most common. (All can be used at the start or end of whole essays as well as to start or end paragraphs.)

OPENINGS

1 Statement of main point (topic).

2 False statement (set up to be argued against).

3 Question (to be answered).

4 Quotation.

5 Definition of something related to main point (topic).

6 Anecdote to lead into subject.

7 Division of subject into parts.

8 Initial characterisation of something by shape, size, use, association, etc (to be followed by more discussion).

9 Two sentences in parallel, eg 'Ali is from India. Britt is from Norway'.

10 Two sentences in contrast, eg 'Electric cars are essential. Gasoline has had its day!'

11 Startling fact.

12 Statistics.

13 Historical information.

14 A pun, eg 'Keep the home fires burning!' as the start of an article on effective heating. (The quotation is a pun because it is a slogan meaning 'Keep the country strong and morale high', used in times of war or other trouble.)

15 Figurative language, eg this opening to an essay on 'Sleep' by J Krishnamurti, *Commentaries on Living*, Victor Gollancz, London, 1956. 'It was a cold winter and the trees were bare. . . . There were very few evergreen trees, and even they felt the cold winds and the frosty nights. . . . The earth was dormant and fallow. . . . What would happen if sleep were denied to us?

1 Statement of main point (topic).
2 False statement (which can now be dismissed in the light of what has been said in the paragraph).
3 Question (pointing in a new direction, or clinching the argument).
4 Quotation.
5 Summary of main points.
6 Anecdote.
7 Two sentences in parallel.
8 Two sentences in contrast.
9 Dramatic or starting conclusion.
10 Poetry (as an interesting summing-up, eg 'A little learning is a dangerous thing'. A Pope, *Essay on Criticism*).
11 Figurative language.
12 Re-statement of opening, either in same words or in paraphrase.

Paragraphs serve the purpose of making reading easier by marking the logical stages in the writer's thoughts and the sub-divisions in his material. There are no rules of length. Short paragraphs are associated with ease of reading, long ones require more concentration. Short paragraphs isolate important details, long paragraphs put a larger amount of information together. In general, the English reader expects each paragraph to make one main point about the topic. He will therefore look for that main point and, if the writer has not signalled it clearly (eg by placing it first in the paragraph, or by using words like 'chiefly', 'most important', 'it is clear that', etc), he will make his own assumptions about what the main point is. Because of this one paragraph-one point convention, it is useful to ask students to follow a series of headings when writing a composition and to use one paragraph for each heading. A subject can thus be divided into its essential components, and students can be shown how to make a series of points in separate paragraphs, supporting each one with some subsidiary material.

The chief problem that teachers face is that students' work

sometimes consists of a string of sentences, each starting with a new line, so that the relationship between main points and subsidiary material is not made clear; or else it consists of a long flow of sentences all in one paragraph continuing for a page or more and, again, not showing the relationship between the different parts of the topic.

Teaching paragraphing needs a two-pronged approach. Firstly, the basic linking devices have to be presented and drilled. This can start at a very early stage as soon as students know enough English to put two sentences together. A sequence like 'Mary is a teacher. She works in my school' is the first stage in learning how to connect sentences properly.

Secondly, logical presentation of ideas should be practised by means of the teaching method suggested in Chapter 1, Section 1.3. That is, a paragraph type is chosen as the teaching objective, and exercises are based on it, with students finally attempting to imitate the model in their own way. Additional help should be given in visual form with plans and outlines showing the structure of the paragraphs. One example was discussed in Chapter 1, page 12. There is further discussion in Chapter 6, Section 6.3–6.3.3, and Chapter 8, Section 8.2.

3.2.1 Classroom application

The guiding principle in applying the suggestions in Section 3.2 is that students must be shown a model of the kind of paragraph they are to write, and then given help in writing their own paragraph to follow the model. The following extract from *Writing in English 2* demonstrates this.

The two couples are friends and wish to meet in Europe. This is the first part of Steve and June's letter to Paul and Eva, suggesting some possible meeting-places.

Exercise 4
Guided writing

Paragraph 1

Paragraph 2
1 Topic
2 Suggestion: time of meeting
3 Result of suggestion
4 Result of 3
5 Benefit of suggestion

18 Connaught Street
London W12
17 May 1982

Dear Paul and Eva,

Wonderful to get your letter with your travel plans! We'd love to meet you in Europe. It may be possible, because we're going to the same countries. However, if we decide to meet, we'll have to change our plans a bit. We can meet in either Paris or Florence.

¹Let's consider Paris first. ²We can meet you there on July 10th and spend two days with you. ³However, if we decide to meet in Paris, June and I will have to go to Lyons before Paris. ⁴That means missing the boat trip. ⁵On the other hand, if we can all meet in Paris, we may be able to share the cost of our car.

Use the information in Exercise 3 to write a third paragraph for the letter, starting with '*Alternatively*', and suggesting a meeting in Florence. Follow the outline showing the structure of Paragraph 2. State the TOPIC, suggest a two-day meeting in Florence, and then describe the change of plans that June and Steve will have to make. Include a 'benefit of suggestion' that is different from the one in Paragraph 2.

Further ideas are in Part Three.

3.3 Linking devices (cohesion)

A writer has to make the relationships between sentences and paragraphs clear to his reader. This section describes the main 'cohesive devices' or connecting words, or linking words or linkers that can be used.

Failure to handle them properly helps to explain why students who perform admirably in standard grammar exercises and appear to have a 'good command of English' nevertheless fail to produce acceptable paragraphs or essays.

Some students limit themselves to the only linking word that is quickly learned because of its high frequency and deceptively easy use, namely 'and', eg

> I would like to live at the coast and it is very beautiful and you can see beautiful views and you can enjoy yourself. When the tide goes out you can walk far into the sea. When you wake up in the morning and have the beautiful smell of the sea. You can be friendly with people and relax and swim in beautiful blue water of the sea.

Other students attempt to show the relationship between ideas, but because they have not been taught cohesion, they produce very strange effects, as in this paragraph, where unsuccessful attempts to link ideas are underlined:

> The US was involved in Cuba after 1898 <u>by trying</u> to help the Cubans to overthrow Spanish rule <u>because</u> Cuba was in American power <u>and after</u> US banned the influence of European power.

There are six ways to establish links between sentences and paragraphs. They are:

1 REFERENCE

Some words do not have any meaning of their own, but take their meaning from some other item which they refer to. Pronouns, demonstratives and some adverbs are the main reference words in English. Thus the word 'he' cannot be understood except by reference to a person, and when it occurs in a written text it serves to relate one sentence to another:

> *The Chancellor* has announced new economy measures. *He* will defend his views tomorrow.

A demonstrative like 'this' may refer to one item or to a whole sentence either preceding it or following it:

> *a* He decided to take an axe. He thought *this* would be needed to cut down the tree.
>
> *b* *This* is what you should do. *You should be very honest.*

Adverbs that create links include 'likewise', 'similarly', 'otherwise' and any others that suggest a comparison with something that has gone before, eg

> Edward jumped over the fence. John tried to do *likewise*.

2 CONJUNCTION

There are four basic conjunction relationships: addition, opposition, cause, and temporal sequence. In their simplest form they are given by: 'and', 'yet', 'so', and 'then'. Other examples are:

> I do not know this person. *Furthermore*, I have never spoken to him.
>
> All the figures have been checked. *In spite of this*, the totals are still wrong.
>
> The price of imports is going up. *As a result*, our inflation is becoming worse.
>
> The evening began with dinner. *After this*, music and dancing were enjoyed in the ballroom.

3 SUBSTITUTION

A substitute word or phrase directly replaces another item in the text which could, in fact, have been used, but is avoided because of repetition.

John *knows* the truth. I think everyone | *does*.
| knows the truth.

These chocolate biscuits are stale.

Get some fresh | *ones*.
| chocolate biscuits.

She thinks *we should take an umbrella*.

I think | *so* too.
| we should take an umbrella.

4 LEXICAL RELATIONSHIPS

This means the links between words themselves. There are many ways in which the choice of words and expressions can unify a piece of writing because of the similarity in meanings among them. The chief ways are the repetition of words, the use of synonyms or near synonyms, and the use of more general words which act as umbrella words for many items in the text, eg

repetion	Last year's increase in *wages* has held down profits. There must be no further *wage* demands.
synonym	I saw a *boy* climbing in the window. The *lad* was not more than ten years old.
general word	Bring a *hammer, saw and some nails*. I hope you have your own *tools*.

5 ELLIPSIS

Ellipsis means the omission of words or phrases, so that the abbreviated structure can only be understood in relation to the full form which must occur somewhere in the surrounding context, eg

It *didn't rain* last month. | It *will* soon.
| (It *will rain* soon).

6 PATTERNING

The use of parallel structures is a common way of linking sentences, eg *It is possible that* your plan *will* succeed. *It is* equally *possible that* it *will* fail.

I have always believed in democracy. And *I have always* said so.

In teaching written English at any level, it is important to include the use of linking devices. Although they enter into normal vocabulary and grammar teaching, they need to be the special focus of some exercises in composition work. The first five linking devices on pages 56 to 58 are described in detail in

Halliday and Hasan (1978), and are summarised in Byrne (1979). (See Bibliography, Section 1.)

3.3.1 Classroom application

The first sample exercise shows how linking words can be taught at elementary level. This is an example of a fairly controlled exercise followed by a slightly less controlled one. It is from a late unit in *Writing in English 1*. It teaches two aspects of cohesion: *a* the use of a pronoun to refer back to a proper noun and *b* the use of the special linking words *and*, *but*, *and then*, *because*, *when*, *so*. This is a rather large number of items for one exercise, but the unit is in fact a revision unit.

The second sample on page 61 illustrates a progression from the use of linking words for sentences to the use of further linkers to create a paragraph. Notice that the exercise assumes that students can put the sentences in logical order, a risky assumption if they have not been familiarised with logical order for this topic. It is from *English in Basic Medical Science* by S McLean, Oxford University Press, Oxford, 1975.

Exercise 1 Join each group of sentences into one, using the words in brackets.
Joining sentences The first one is finished for you.
    Change 'Roger Green' to *he*, except after *and* and *but* because you can omit it then.
    In **d**, omit 'Roger Green will', and in **j**, omit 'The parachute' after *and*.
    Write the story in three paragraphs.

Paragraph 1

a Roger Green is a parachutist. (AND)
   Roger Green has jumped many times.
   Roger Green is a parachutist and has jumped many times.

b Roger Green is going to make his first free fall jump today.
   (AND) Roger Green will get a badge.

c Roger Green is going to jump from the plane (BUT)
   Roger Green is not going to open his parachute immediately.

d Roger Green is going to fall for a few minutes. (AND THEN)
   Roger Green will open it.

e Parachuting is dangerous. (BECAUSE)
   If your parachute does not open
   You will die. (WHEN)
   You hit the ground.

Paragraph 2

f Roger Green has packed his parachute. (AND)
   Roger Green is getting into the plane.

g Now the plane is at 1000 metres. (SO)
   Roger Green is near the door. (AND)
   Roger Green is going to jump out.

h Roger Green has spread out his arms and legs. (AND)
   Roger Green is falling quickly.

i Roger Green has pulled the rip cord. (AND)
   Roger Green is waiting for the parachute to open.

Paragraph 3

j Suddenly the parachute opens. (AND)
   The parachute is floating above him.

k Roger Green is coming down slowly. (AND)
   Roger Green is landing safely.

l Roger Green has made his first free fall jump.

Exercise 2
Joining sentences

Now join these sentences. Make one paragraph.

m The parachute has not opened. (SO)
   Roger Green is pulling the cord again. (BUT)
   Nothing is happening.

n Roger Green cannot see anything. (BECAUSE)
   Roger Green is moving so fast.

o Suddenly Roger Green hits the ground. (AND)
   Everything is black.

p An ambulance has rushed Roger Green to hospital. (BUT)
   Roger Green has made his first and last free fall jump.

IV Guided writing
STAGE 1 *Sentence building*

Join each of the groups of sentences below into one long sentence, using the additional words printed in capital letters above each group. Omit words printed in italics and put relative clauses in the places marked by dots. Make whatever changes you think are necessary in the punctuation of the sentences.

EXAMPLE

    WHICH

    The weighing machine ..... is one of the doctor's most useful tools.
    The weighing machine can be found in any clinic.
    It is used for assessing the general health of his patients.

= The weighing machine which can be found in any clinic is one of the doctor's most useful tools for assessing the general health of his patients.

1 WHICH
    Oedema ..... is a typical feature of many cardiac, renal and liver diseases.
    Oedema is due to an increase in the extracellular water.

2 WITH/AND
    The body is composed of different compartments.
    Each *compartment* has a different function.
    These compartments are affected differently by different diseases.

3 THAT
    It must always be kept in mind.
    The body is not a uniform mass.

4   IF/THEN
    The size of the increase in the supporting tissue equals the
    size of the reduction in the other two compartments.
    The total body weight remains constant.

5   TOO/A/TO BE
    The weighing machine is *a* crude tool.
    It cannot be an accurate guide to health.

6   AND/BUT/WHICH
    There is a reduction in the cell mass.
    There is a reduction in the energy reserve.
    There is an increase in the supporting tissue .....
    This increase is caused by oedema.

STAGE 2 *Paragraph building*
Add the following material to the sentences indicated:
    write 'for example' at the beginning of sentence 1
    write 'it' instead of 'the body' in sentence 2
    add 'however' to sentence 3
    add 'in cases like these' to the beginning of sentence 5
    write 'in wasting diseases too,' at the beginning of sentence 6.

Rewrite the six sentences in a logical order to make a paragraph, and include the example as the first sentence of the
paragraph.

When you have written your paragraph, re-read it and make
sure the sentences are presented in a logical order. Give the
paragraph a suitable title. (Make any changes that you think are
necessary, but remember that sentences can often be arranged in
more than one way.)

Further ideas are in Part Three.

4 Style

4.1 The four major styles

Traditionally, four major styles of writing are named: *narrative*, which presents a sequence of events (though not necessarily in chronological order); *description*, which gives an account of the features of things, people, and concepts; *exposition*, which outlines and details factual information; and *argument* which presents one or more approaches to issues and problems.

Although it is usually better to teach these styles separately, most writing probably consists of a mixture of two or more of them. Academic writing, for instance, requires exposition and argument, but also narrative (to give the order of historical events or the events in an experiment) and description (of people in history or objects in science). Fiction, which is mainly narrative, also normally includes description and often has some exposition and argument, perhaps in dialogue. Tourist information is mainly description, but occasionally includes exposition and narrative. Journalism accommodates all styles—narrative of events, description of people, places and things, expository articles on scientific or other topical matters, and argument in letters, editorials and special articles.

The chief difference between the four styles is in the presentation of ideas following different logical functions as discussed in Chapter 2, Section 2.3. Thus, narrative is associated mainly with No. 3, sequence of events, with some occurrence of No. 1, description, and No. 4, cause-effect. Description depends mainly on No. 1, features, and No. 2, processes, with some occurrence of No. 6, similarities, and No. 7, contrasts. Exposition associates mainly with No. 8, generalisations, but often includes most of the others. Argument is largely either No. 9, hypothesis, or No. 10, for and against, but generally includes some expository writing as well.

Other features of style that can be observed are: contrasts between tense-forms, cause-effect relations, prepositions and verbs of motion, etc in *narrative*; adjective sequences, spatial prepositions, etc in *description*; general nouns and definition structures in *exposition*; and superlatives, modals and logical terms in *argument*. Such features of style can easily be picked out of selected samples, and should be practised in connection with them.

4.1.1 Classroom application

The sample opposite is part of a unit introducing argument at elementary level in *Writing in English 1*.

4.2 Formality

The formal-informal distinction is a matter of degree. It can be envisaged as a range of possibilities, from the most informal at one end, through neutral all-purpose style in the middle, to the very formal at the other end. A writer's choice will depend entirely on what attitude he feels he should adopt towards his reader. Most learners of English will be quite used to operating different levels of formality in their own languages, since this is

This is a poster.

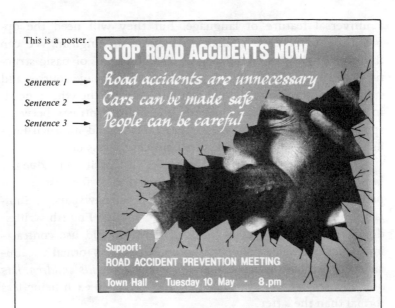

Sentence 1 →
Sentence 2 →
Sentence 3 →

STOP ROAD ACCIDENTS NOW

Road accidents are unnecessary
Cars can be made safe
People can be careful

Support:
ROAD ACCIDENT PREVENTION MEETING
Town Hall · Tuesday 10 May · 8.pm

Exercise 1 The poster contains an argument. Sentence 1 is the main point.
Completion Sentences 2 and 3 support the argument.
Complete these arguments using the words from the list:

.... is .... People *can* ....
.... Marriages ....
be made ....

| be |
| unnecessary |
| happy together |
| divorce |
| can |
| better |

.... is not .... The Church forbids
.... is very .... for children.

| divorce |
| it |
| damaging |
| right |

Further ideas are in Part Three.

a universal feature of language, but they will need the opportunity to observe similar distinctions in English. We can think of English as containing a 'common core' of basic structures and vocabulary. This is used in most language courses and suits the kind of neutral style that students, on the whole, need. In addition to the common core, there are contrasts between spoken and written English, between formal and informal English, and between polite and more familiar expressions.

Most informal writing is of the kind that is written to give the impression of the writer talking to his reader, for instance in personal letters, advertisements and popular newspapers. Similarly, dialogues in stories and plays are spoken English written down. For this kind of writing, students should use contractions, short sentences, short paragraphs, and less formal vocabulary. English has numerous parallel words like *kids/children*, *lots of/many*, *tell/inform*, *come in/enter*, the former in each being less formal than the latter.

Students should learn to distinguish such writing from the kind that is intended for strangers (eg in most business correspondence) or for a wider, unknown audience (as in essays and most academic writing). In this type of writing, we use more impersonal language, such as the passive rather than the active voice, or the introductory *it* (eg 'It is important to remember that...'). We also use more 'traditional' grammar, for instance *whom* in relative clauses. Compare:

Mr Jones is the man whom I must see	*formal, written*
Mr Jones is the man who I must see ⎫	*informal,*
Mr Jones is the man I must see ⎭	*spoken*

Another example is the placing of the preposition which tends to come at the end in less formal style. Compare:

In what city do you live?	*formal, written*
What city do you live in?	*informal, spoken*

Other distinctions in vocabulary between formal and informal style include the contrast between informal phrasal verbs (eg *find out*) and their more formal equivalents (eg *discover*), between more formal noun phrases (eg 'After his sister's marriage...') and less formal clauses (eg 'After his sister married...'), and between words of Anglo-Saxon origin (eg *begin*) which are felt to be less formal than those of French, Latin, or Greek origin (eg *commence*).

Formal writing is of course more polite than informal writing and we might, for instance, use 'Would you be good enough to send the parcel as soon as possible?' instead of 'Send the parcel straight away, will you?', or 'May I suggest a different approach?' instead of 'I don't think we should do that'.

The present trend is towards less formal style in contexts such as newspapers, public forms and notices, and business correspondence, where a generation or two ago only a very formal style was permitted. If teachers wish to give their students competence in this area, then they must help them to develop a sensitivity to formality through reading samples of different varieties of English.

4.2.1 Classroom application

Probably the most effective exercise is one that shows how the very same set of facts can be expressed informally or formally. Students need to be first shown a clearly contrasting pair of passages, and then asked to convert a passage in the style of one of that pair to the style of the other. Similar work could be done at an earlier stage in the learning of English, especially in contrasting formal and informal letters, or informal dialogue with more formal prose versions of the same information. This is an exercise from *Writing in English 1*.

Exercise 1
Paragraph writing

A girl is missing and Constable Peach is trying to find her. He needs information and asks her room-mate questions. Read the conversation between Constable Peach and the missing girl's room-mate.

Then make a list of sentences with information, like the list in Unit 1, Exercise 1. Do not use contractions, change them to full forms. eg What's → What is ... She's → She is ...

Then use the sentences to write a paragraph as in Unit 1, Exercise 3. Constable Peach writes this paragraph in his police report.

Constable Peach	Would you please tell me about the missing girl?
Jennifer	Well, Elizabeth is a teacher.
Constable Peach	What's her full name?
Jennifer	Elizabeth Grace Bandela.
Constable Peach	What colour's her hair?
Jennifer	She's got black hair.
Constable Peach	How old is she?
Jennifer	About twenty-six.
Constable Peach	Where was she born?
Jennifer	In Lagos. Now she lives in London.
Constable Peach	Do you know her height? Colour of eyes?
Jennifer	I think she has brown eyes. She's 1.68m tall.
Constable Peach	Any children?
Jennifer	Oh, no. She's single.

Further ideas are in Part Three.

4.3 Emotive tone

This refers both to the effect that the writer wants to have on the reader (eg to persuade him of something) and to the impression he may wish the reader to gain about him (eg that the writer is angry or protective, etc). It is not an aspect of writing that will have great priority for most foreign learners of English who, at least at elementary and intermediate levels, will probably find a safe neutral tone sufficient for what they write. Nevertheless, it is of value to demonstrate differences of tone so that students learn to recognise them to some extent, even before they have the language ability to produce them.

Tone is affected by a number of different factors in writing. Probably the most important is the choice of what kind of statement is made. For instance, to sound friendly one might choose to make a suggestion, whereas in the same circumstances one would choose to give a command if one didn't mind sounding angry. So the tone of 'If I were you, I'd wash the car' (a suggestion) can be more friendly than 'Go and wash the car' (a command).

Other factors are the order of presentation by which one can choose to give prominence to certain details of a subject (eg emphasise the consequences of an action rather than its causes), the sentence length (eg short sentences are often used in narrative to give an effect of speed, tension or excitement), the use of specific examples instead of over-all generalisations (the former gives a more authentic and believable effect in many cases), the choice of words (eg certain words have pleasant associations while others have unpleasant ones: compare *a juicy apple/a wrinkled apple*, *a warm voice/a cold voice*), and the use of writing devices like exclamation marks, underlining, capital letters, etc.

As is the case with the distinction between formal and informal style, a feeling for effect cannot be taught by simple rules. It has to develop over a period of exposure to many different examples of language usage. The best approach to emotive tone is therefore demonstration, in context, of contrasting examples, eg a polite letter *vs* an angry, rude letter, an objective description of a political meeting *vs* a biased description of the same meeting, and so on.

To involve students in writing with different emotive effects, it is necessary to create a realistic context in which the effect is necessary and believable. In the absence of any real need to write, say, a love-letter or complaint in English, the teacher has to prepare a group activity or game in which a stimulating context is established.

4.3.1 Classroom application

A useful source of emotive language is the English of advertising. The sample here is part of a unit from *Writing in English 2*. The focus is on the use of comparatives and superlatives to achieve a favourable effect on the reader.

Exercise 1
Word Study

(i) Which advertisement { gives more facts?
{ sounds more exciting?

(ii) Count the number of times the word *more* appears in the first advertisement. Does it appear in the second?

(iii) Count the times the words *good*, *better*, *best* appear in the first advertisement. Do they appear in the second?

(iv) Find the words *exciting*, *special fascination*, *expertise*, *special*, *individual attention*, *perfect*, *greatest*, *hand-picked*, in the first advertisement. Do they give the reader more facts than in the second advertisement? What do they add to the advertisement?

YUGOSLAVIA

Holidays in Yugoslavia, Greece, Romania and Austria

This year is the time to choose Yugotours. Because this year Yugotours offer four countries, twelve holidays, five different types of service and value for money.

We now arrange different holidays in three new countries. There will be sea and sun, lakes and mountains, lonely islands, coach tours and cruises.

We have experts and we give you individual attention. We have a choice of five flights, and eight holiday resorts. We have inspected all the hotels. None costs more than £40 per night for one person for bed and breakfast. We try very hard to keep to our arrangements with you.

If you write to us, we will send you our brochure.

Further ideas are in Part Three.

PART THREE

WRITING EXERCISES

Introduction

Even a casual inspection of the many workbooks and course-books that offer composition exercises will reveal a bewildering variety of types. Some exercises are called 'guided', some are called 'controlled', some use substitution frames, others follow question-answer procedures, yet others use picture-matching, and so on. There is an apparently endless stream of exercise types. A teacher can be forgiven for feeling at a loss how to evaluate the various suggestions or how to select appropriate work for his class.

It is therefore useful to have a simple classification of the kinds of exercises that can be used for composition teaching. The Chart on p 77 shows that classification in summary. Chapter 5 gives examples of familiarisation exercises while Chapters 6, 7 and 8 deal with the other types, though not all options can be exemplified in the space available in this book. Teachers can use the classification both as a way of judging any existing exercises they find in workbooks, and as a blueprint for writing their own supplementary exercises. (The sequence familiarisation-controlled-guided-free must not be equated with a grading scheme. As was pointed out in Chapter 1, Section 3, Teaching method, it is a progression that can be usefully followed through a lesson unit at any level of language ability.)

The Chart is divided into three main sections which reflect the three main factors that influence the design of a writing exercise:

1   TYPE: This indicates the purpose of the exercise, ie it in-

dicates what the student is being asked to do (to identify something, to evaluate something, etc).

2 TECHNIQUE: This indicates what procedures are being used in the exercise, ie it indicates the activity the student will be engaged in (underlining, matching, comparing words, pictures, passages, etc).

The Types and Techniques can be cross-matched. Most Types can be done through the use of any of the Techniques. For instance, the first Type, 'identifying', can be used with the first Technique, 'underlining', in an 'identifying by underlining' exercise in which the student shows that he can identify something, perhaps linking words, by underlining them in a given passage. If the students are asked to match, say, three passages all using *he* and three different pictures of males, each picture relating to one passage only, then the exercise is a simple 'identifying by matching' one. If they are given four passages, two of which use *he* and two of which use *she*, and asked to match them against two pictures of males, then the exercise relies a little more on discrimination, that is still basically 'identifying by matching'.

An example of 'identifying by comparing' would be one in which students are given two passages that have some similarities (eg similar topic) and some differences of style. They are then asked to compare the passages and try to decide where each came from, either very loosely (eg extracts from a newspaper), or more precisely (eg from *David Copperfield*). An example of 'identifying by multiple choice' would be one in which students are given a paragraph and then asked to indicate which logical function it has by checking the correct one in a list of possible functions.

Thus, starting from the first Type, 'identifying', we can work our way through the list of Techniques, finding a way of using each Technique for each Type. Then we can return to the next Type, 'evaluating', and go through the list of Techniques again in the same way and so forth through the entire chart.

3 CUE: At the same time as we have been relating Types and Techniques, we have, in fact, already been considering Cues: pictures, written passages, or multiple-choice questions. Virtually any of the Cues is suitable as a stimulus for any of the Types and Techniques. As a general principle teachers should aim for as great a variety as possible.

At one end of the scale is a complete activity in which the whole class participates and which provides the stimulus and all the information needed for a related writing activity. For instance, after an outing deliberately chosen to be informative (perhaps a visit to a local museum), the students could describe it for the school magazine, or compose a letter of thanks to the person who welcomed them, or perhaps write an essay based on information they collected. Equally full background information can be given by reading about a subject, and this reading can be either in English or in the mother tongue if all that is required is the content.

At the other end of the scale are several cues which by their nature are simply suggestive and do not actually provide the material to write about. Music, noises, or essay titles are more open to a wide variety of interpretation than other cues. With these, the teacher might aim to stimulate the students' imagination and initiative, but foreign language students should obviously not be expected to produce 'creative' writing of the same standard as in their native language.

Any cue can be useful at any level of English. For example, given a bus-timetable, elementary students could write a short note to a friend who needed to know when to catch a bus, and they might even use a timetable in their native tongue to get the information. More advanced students, however, could write fuller details of alternatives taken from the timetable.

The exercises that are suggested in the four chapters of this Part are numbered throughout.

WRITING EXERCISES

TYPE : what is being done

FAMILIARISATION	CONTROLLED WRITING	GUIDED WRITING	FREE WRITING
Identifying	Combining	Completion	Expansion
Evaluating	Substitution	Reproduction	Completion
		Compression	Translation
		Paraphrase	Transposition
			Pictures
			Games

TECHNIQUE : how it is being done

underlining
matching
comparing
multiple choice
copying
re-ordering
correcting/improving
using plans and outlines

CUE : how it is stimulated

AUDIO—VISUAL	WRITING (English or mother tongue)
activity (incl. game)	full reading on topic
events	selected reading
class discussion	outlines of essays
listening comprehension	charts and tabulations
(talks,	essay titles
plays, etc)	
objects	
people	
pictures	
maps	
noises	
music	

5 Familiarisation

5.1 General principles

The first type of exercise on the chart on page 77, *familiarisation*, means preparing students for actual writing by demonstrating one or other of the skills that are to be practised. Since reading alone is not sufficient preparation—ie students often fail to notice the important aspect of what they read—familiarisation requires specific exercises. See Chapter 1, Section 3, Teaching method, for a discussion of how familiarisation exercises fit into a lesson procedure.

One of the keys to good familiarisation work is to give contrasting examples wherever possible. For instance, to teach the difference between speaking and writing, the teacher can let the class hear a spoken invitation (perhaps on tape or in a film if possible), and then read a written invitation (not a written version of what was spoken!). Or again, they could listen to a brief verbal explanation of something (perhaps part of a science lecture), and then read an explanation of the same facts in a textbook.

If the teacher wants to demonstrate a spatial description, he can use a description of the layout of a school and another of a hospital. The logical pattern the two passages have in common then stands out more clearly than if only one passage had been used:

Our school *is on* three *floors*. *The ground floor contains* an assembly hall, a gymnasium, *and* the teachers' offices. *The upper* two *floors consist of* classrooms *and* science laboratories.

The hospital *is on* five *floors*. *The ground floor contains* the casualty department *and* the out-patient admissions. *The other* four *floors are* in-patient wards *and* operating theatres.

Another kind of demonstration by contrast involves showing the consequences of writing something in the wrong way. For instance, to demonstrate the need for logical order in instructions, the teacher can prepare some confusing ones and ask students to try to carry them out, eg confusing instructions to draw an unfamiliar object on the board, or to make a cardboard house, or to perform a mime or play a game. Then, when the instructions are seen to be inadequate, he can draw on the students' observations to improve them. Exercises like these focus the students' attention on the practical value of what they are doing.

The remaining sections of this chapter describe the two main types of familiarisation—identifying and evaluating.

5.2 Familiarisation by identifying

The principle behind 'identifying' exercises is to stimulate close reading and an awareness of the features of writing. The aim is to have students demonstrate that they have understood the teaching point by identifying something (though they are not necessarily called upon to make their understanding analytically explicit).

In most cases the teacher should give a brief demonstration of what is required, and then let the class carry on, either individually or in groups or as a whole class responding to his questions. For instance, in teaching the use of logical connectors (linking words), the teacher points out the first one, explaining its meaning, and then asks the class to underline others. He could cue this exercise in different ways, depending on the level of the class. For an advanced class he might only need to say 'Underline the other logical connectors', but for a lower level class he might help by saying something like 'Find a word that means *but*', or he might even use the native language and ask the class to find the English equivalents in the passage. It does not matter if the teaching point is not fully understood at this stage since familiarisation will be followed by controlled and guided practice which will clarify it further.

5.2.1 Identifying by underlining

1 Linking words   Underline pronouns and draw a line back to the nouns they refer to.
2 Linking words   Find synonyms or near synonyms, and also repetitions of the same word, and underline all of them.
3 Logical functions   Find and underline expressions like 'however', 'consequently' and 'as a result':
4 Paragraphing   Underline anything that could be omitted. (The teacher prepares passages with deliberately inserted irrelevant material.)
5 Presentation of ideas   Underline key words and phrases. This is a good first step before writing notes or a summary.
6 Paragraphs   Find and underline the topic sentence of each paragraph.

In all of these examples, the cue was simply the written passage. But further assistance could be given if a picture, chart or table helped to make the work clearer. For instance, in relation to No. 4, if the given passage described a travel route, then a map of that route would help students to judge which parts of the passage were irrelevant.

5.2.2 Identifying by matching

In matching exercises, students show that they can identify (ie respond to) something by observing relationships either between two pieces of writing or between writing and another cue.

7 *Subject matter* Match filled-in application forms, tabulations, graphs, family trees, etc with passages containing the same facts.

8 *Subject matter* Given a number of passages and a list of topic headings (such that each topic heading relates to only one passage), match them.

9 *Logical function: classification using general and particular terms* Match particular terms from a passage with general terms in a given list (eg match words like 'furniture' with words like 'table' in a passage), or *vice versa*.

10 *Logical functions* Match expressions from passages with logical functions (eg 'as a result' and 'because of this' would match with 'cause/effect'; while 'then' and 'meanwhile' would match with 'sequence of events').

11 *Description* Students bring objects to class (eg tin-opener, key-ring, postcards), or draw objects or animals (perhaps imaginary ones), or perform a mime or hold a conversation. The teacher writes a description of each, and then asks students to match the description with the items. Later, the same 'game' can be used for writing practice if the students write the descriptions themselves.

12 *Description contrasted with instruction* The teacher prepares pairs of passages: (i) a description of an item (ii) a set of brief instructions for its use. Each passage is on a separate piece of paper. Students take passages at random. Each student then

matches an action to his passage. If a student has a descriptive passage, he draws the item; if he has an instruction passage he has to get the item and show that he can follow the instructions either by using the item or miming if it is not available.

13 Description (spatial) Match descriptions of city lay-outs with corresponding maps. The written descriptions can be used to teach the difference between terms like 'radiating from the centre' and 'concentric'.

14 Narrative sequence Matching can also involve re-ordering. For example, a strip cartoon showing a story can be matched with passages or sentences (each of which relates to only one picture in the strip) given to the class in random order. Alternatively, the sentences or passages can be presented in the right order and the pictures mixed up.

15 Exposition (instructional) The teacher prepares some short passages of instructions for simple activities, eg cutting paper into certain shapes, or performing simple physical exercises, etc. Each instruction differs from the others in only minor details, eg 'raise both arms after jumping twice' *vs* 'raise both arms before jumping twice'. One student (or group) at a time is shown an instruction passage and does the actions. The passages are then mixed up on a table and students find the passage that matches what they did, demonstrating thereby that they can respond to slight differences in wording.

16 Formality Match passages in formal and informal style with a given list of persons (or pictures of contexts) likely to be associated with them. Formal writing would associate with a textbook, for instance, while informal writing would associate with a popular magazine.

17 Style Match given words or phrases with synonyms or near synonyms in given passages. This exercise can be used to teach paraphrasing for summarising, or to show differences in style, eg if the given passages are in plain factual style, and the list of words or phrases are emotive, this could lead to a writing exercise in which the emotive terms are substituted for the plain ones, thus making the passage emotive.

18   *Argument*   Match argument passages with summaries of their main points, or with slogans that could arise out of them, with pictures to illustrate them, or with persons who would be likely to agree with them.

All of the matching exercises can be made more challenging if distractors are added, ie if the two sets of items that have to be matched are not equal in number. One item from one list will be the 'odd man out'.

5.2.3   Identifying by comparing

As was pointed out earlier, it is easiest to identify contrasting items against a common background. Thus the differences between the four paragraphs in Set A on the next page can be clearly seen against the background of identical facts which they all contain. Passages *a*, *b*, and *c*, convey the same information in different paragraph arrangements, while passage *d* follows the arrangement of *a*, but is in informal language.

In Set B the similarities between the two paragraphs stand out against the contrasting background, ie the different subject-matter. Both passages have the same structure signalled by the same linking words 'On the one hand', 'if', 'on the other hand', 'this would', 'moreover', 'However', 'if'.

Observation of similarities and differences between passages can be the basis of many kinds of exercises.

19   *Linking terms*   Identify similar uses of words like 'and', 'in addition' and 'besides', or 'because', 'since' and 'therefore', in different passages.

20 *Communicative functions*   Identify the different functions of two descriptions of the same object, eg a description of a car in an advertisement and in a technical manual.

21 *Emotive tone*   Identify the different tones of two otherwise similar accounts of the same event, eg a coincidence described by a person for whom it was lucky and then by a person for whom it was unlucky.

SET A

a   Crime does not pay. Most, if not all, criminals are caught sooner or later. They find their punishment greatly outweighs the gains of their transgression. Even if they are not caught early, the strain of avoiding the law is sure to take its toll.

b   Most, if not all, criminals are caught sooner or later. Then they find that their punishment greatly outweighs the gains of their transgression. So crime does not pay. Even if they are not caught early, the strain of avoiding the law is sure to take its toll.

c   Most, if not all, criminals are caught sooner or later. Then they find that their punishment greatly outweighs the gains of their transgression. Even if they are not caught early, the strain of avoiding capture is sure to take its toll. So crime does not pay.

d   Crime really isn't worth the trouble at all, you know. Most criminals, and I daresay all of them, get caught sooner or later, and their gains from their wrongdoing don't make up to them for the punishment they get. And, as for those who don't get caught early, they have the strain of keeping clear of the law— that gets them down in the end, too.

On the one hand, if the government increases taxes, there will be more public works. *On the other hand*, citizens would spend less. *This* would harm the economy. *Moreover*, it would lower public confidence in the economy. *However*, if the government arranged a drop in prices, the situation would improve.

On the one hand, if Hamlet kills his uncle, his father's ghost will be revenged. *On the other hand*, the court would be in an uproar. *This* would endanger Hamlet's own position as Prince. *Moreover*, it would put his mother to public shame. However, if Hamlet killed his uncle secretly, there would be even more confusion at Elsinore.

5.2.4 Identifying by multiple choice questions (MCQs)

Although MCQs are mostly used for testing, they are also a helpful teaching device. They have the advantage of speed and since they do not require students to write, they are ideal for familiarisation.

22 Linking words Given a passage of two paragraphs, students have to place a circle around *a* or *b* or *c* to show which one functions as the link between them:

      a Moreover
      b On the other hand
      c By contrast

23 Paragraphs Given a paragraph and told that one sentence is missing, students decide whether the missing sentence would have been:

      a the topic sentence
      b a support sentence
      c an exemplification
      d a re-statement

24 Variety of writing Given a passage, students indicate where it probably came from:

  a   university textbook
  b   a popular magazine
  c   a student's lecture notes

5.2.5 Identifying by re-ordering

Re-ordering either jumbled words or jumbled sentences can be a challenging exercise. It can be used to help students identify the structure of a sentence or paragraph by putting the parts together. But they need the clear guidance of a plan or model to do so.

25 Logical functions This is an example of a complex exercise in two parts. *Part 1:* students read a passage of about six sentences describing three different stages of a process, eg of a jet engine: air intake, combustion, thrust. They then match each of the three stages with a picture by writing the technical name under the appropriate picture. *Part 2:* students are given six new sentences describing air intake, combustion and thrust. The sentences are paraphrases of those in the original passage and are given in jumbled order. Students sort the new sentences into groups according to which stages of the process they refer to, and then write them out in the correct order to form a new passage describing the jet engine.

26 Paragraphs Given a paragraph to use as model, students re-order jumbled sentences about a different topic to form a paragraph of the same structural type as the model. A paragraph plan can be given to help them.

5.2.6 Identifying by using plans and outlines

Plans and outlines are described in Chapter 8 Section 8.2.

27 *Paragraph and essay structure* Students write a plan to show that they can identify the main points in a given piece of writing.

28 *Logical function* Students complete a diagram or chart to show that they can follow the presentation of ideas in a passage, for instance they can label a diagram of an engine after reading a description of it, or complete a chart showing a process like the growing and making of cotton after reading about it.

5.3 Familiarisation by evaluating

The purpose of evaluative exercises is to make students discriminate between successful and unsuccessful writing. They are often similar to identifying, but with the right emphasis they should in the long run have a beneficial effect on the students' critical approach to their own work.

5.3.1 Evaluating by underlining

29 *Style* Students underline powerful metaphors, or other stylistic features. Alternatively, underline weak metaphors.

30 *Relevance* Students underline irrelevant material (the teacher has to prepare passages for this).

5.3.2 Evaluating by matching

31 Description Students match the more logical of two passages with a given picture, object, etc.

32 Paragraphs Students match the more appropriate of two (or more) opening or closing sentences with a given, incomplete paragraph.

33 Summaries Students match the better of two summaries with the full version. The summaries can be prepared either by the teacher or by the students.

5.3.3 Evaluating by comparing

34 Paragraphs Given two versions of the same paragraph, one having the topic sentence first, the other having it last, students decide which order is more effective.

35 Argument Given two versions of the same paragraph, one using concrete details effectively, the other being vague because of lack of detail, students comment on the merits of either.

36 Style Students compare more or less effective writing in terms of interest *vs* monotony, tension *vs* anti-climax, bias *vs* impartiality.

37 Formality Given two versions of the same passage, one having mixed levels of formality and the other being an improved version, students decide which is better and why.

38 Emotive tone Given several passages, some of which contain jarring words or phrases that are out of tone, students choose the best passage and improve the others.

5.3.4 Evaluating by MCQs

39 Essay structure Given a short essay with the final paragraph missing, students choose an appropriate one from two or three alternatives prepared by the teacher. The choice might be determined by the linking words, the degree of formality, the tone, etc.

40 Formality Given a passage with words missing, students choose from a list of alternatives and put words in the blanks to suit the formality of the passage.

41 Logical function Paragraphs are followed by MCQs like:

a   This paragraph is effective because it
  (i)   starts with a generalisation.
  (ii)   has good support sentences.
  (iii) has a generalisation and support sentences.

or

b   This paragraph is effective because it
  (i)   follows chronological order.
  (ii)   has short sentences.
  (iii) shows the time sequence with linking words.

5.3.5 Evaluating by re-ordering

42 Paragraphs Students choose the best organised paragraph from three given, one of which is well-organised and the other two of which are in some degree of confusion. They re-order the bad paragraphs. (The best way of preparing confused paragraphs is to take well-written ones and, without altering any words, shift the sentences around at random.)

5.3.6 Evaluating by correcting/improving

43 Logical function Given two or more paragraphs, students find the one with a sentence missing. The teacher must prepare a paragraph with an obvious indication that a sentence is missing, eg a statement like 'This was the result' requires that the result is then described. Students re-write the passage and insert a sentence as required, perhaps cued by pictures, lists of possible sentences, etc.

44 Paragraphs Given a very long paragraph, students decide whether and where it could be divided. There should be clear markers for division, eg 'On the other hand'.

6 Controlled writing

6.1 General principles

Whereas familiarisation exercises are designed to show students the kind of writing they will produce in a lesson, controlled exercises give writing practice. They are devised so that students have virtually no freedom to make mistakes.

The two types of controlled exercises—combining and substitution—lend themselves to a great variety of techniques and cues. The latter is the most fruitful and is given the most space.

6.2 Controlled writing by combining

Combining exercises can join words into sentences, sentences into paragraphs or paragraphs into essays. They are on the brink of production, since they involve students in constructing some writing. But since all elements are given, they are very simple to do and can be stimulated by almost any cue. Only a few examples from a vast range are given here.

6.2.1 Combining by matching

45 Description of process Students are given picture(s) to show stages in a process, and then two columns of sentences, so that one sentence from one column has to be joined with one sentence from the other column to make a compound sentence related to a stage in the process.

46 Paragraphs Following a strip picture story, or a large picture showing a story, students are given lists of simple sentences arranged in general groups with one or two linking words per group. Each group of simple sentences has to be joined into one compound or complex sentence using the linking words. The resulting sentences make a paragraph.

6.2.2 Combining by re-ordering

47 Listening comprehension The teacher reads a story or essay, and then the students are given the sentences from it in the wrong order. They re-arrange them to re-produce the original. This can be helped by the use of linking words in the original.

48 Narrative Sentences are elicited from the class, perhaps by free association with random words called by the teacher: the words have been chosen in relation to a theme or context that is suitable for a piece of writing. Then students are asked to use their imagination to put these sentences together in a story. Depending on the sentences, the teacher will have to allow a few limited changes to be made, and will have to restrict the additional material that can be put in.

49 Sentences or paragraphs Several sentences or paragraphs are on slips of paper, and have to be arranged on one large sheet prepared by the teacher with suitable linking words written on it so that the slips of paper have to be correctly placed. Thus:

6.2.3 Combining by using plans and outlines

Any exercise in combining given sentences into paragraphs, or given paragraphs into essays, can be assisted with a plan of the whole paragraph or whole essay that is to be built up. See the discussion of plans and outlines in Section 6.3.3, and Chapter 8, Section 8.2.

6.3 Controlled writing by substitution

The substitution frame is commonly used for structure exercises. (See Haycraft 1978 for a useful discussion of substitution frames.) The basic technique of letting students make sentences by using words presented in columns showing the pattern of the sentences can be extended to the teaching of writing skills. Just as words can be varied within one fixed sentence pattern, so can sentences be varied within one paragraph pattern, and paragraphs within one essay pattern. The writing that results might be called 'controlled imitation'.

The belief that one way to learn to write well is to imitate models is not a new one. But free imitation leads to too many errors. Indeed, many students, if asked to imitate a model, do not know what features to focus on, ie they do not know what to imitate or how to go about it. Substitution exercises pinpoint the items to be imitated and control the students' work. Wherever some choices are allowed in the substitution, there is an element of creativity that takes it beyond mechanical practice.

Substitution work can be used for direct imitation or for contrastive imitation. In direct imitation, the teacher presents a model (paragraph, letter, essay, etc) and then provides the new words, sentences, paragraphs, etc that are to be substituted for some of those in the model. The teacher can indicate where the substitute items are to go by underlining parts of the model, or by setting the model out in a conventional substitution frame, by eliciting ideas from the class, etc. Of course the new items must be such that an acceptable new piece will be produced.

In contrastive imitation, the new items must be such that a different piece results from the substitutions, eg it may have a different tense, or a different point of view (third person instead of first).

Substitution work must be well prepared. Students should be shown exactly where to make substitutions. If the teacher asks them to find their own new words or phrases he should always suggest an appropriate topic since not all subject-matter will be suitable and a great deal of time is often wasted while students try to think of new topics.

Although substitution has been included in this chapter on Controlled writing, it can in fact provide a bridge to Guided writing (Chapter 7) in which there is a greater element of choice. In a totally controlled substitution exercise, all items are given and students are told which slots to fit them into. In a guided substitution exercise, new items may be given but students are not told where to slot them. In a still less controlled exercise, only the frame and a new topic are given and students have to find their own new items.

Substitution frames are very similar to plans and outlines. See Chapter 8, Section 8.2.

6.3.1 Substitution of words and phrases in sentences

The easiest way of utilising substitution frame exercises for composition work (at any level of language ability) is to build up from substitution in isolated sentences to combining these sentences in paragraphs and then going on to longer substitution involving whole paragraphs at a time.

For instance, having started with drills like:

The girls The boys	in the class in the team	speak English play football	very well too roughly

and

Their teacher Their manager	often sometimes	praises them stops them

students can be shown how to put these and one or two further sentences together to build up short paragraphs:

> The girls in the class speak English very well. Their teacher often praises them and is sure that they will pass their examinations. However, they must not stop working.

> The boys in the team play football too roughly. Their manager often stops them, but is confident that they will win their matches. However, they must not stop training.

Such paragraphs already associated with a substitution exercise can then be used for further paragraph writing. Students are given more words and phrases to fit into the slots and produce another paragraph, eg

> The girls in the school do gymnastics most beautifully. Their Head often watches them and is certain that they can win their competitions. However, they must not stop practising.

In such exercises the substitutions may be word for word, or phrase for phrase. For instance, the two paragraphs in Group 1 on the next page show fairly strict word for word substitution, while those in Group 2 are freer. The phrases 'get up' and 'get to school', or 'he doesn't wake up' and 'he has time' are structurally different, but one can reasonably substitute for the other in these paragraphs.

Group 1

The cat is a smaller animal than a dog. It is covered with soft fur. It is a clean animal and often washes itself with its tongue. Most cats like to drink milk. They often try to catch birds. Young cats are called kittens.

A bus is a larger vehicle than a taxi. It is built with many seats. It is a powerful vehicle and often surprises people with its speed. All buses stop to take passengers. They often speed to keep schedules. Big buses are called double-deckers.

Group 2

Jack gets up at seven o'clock in the morning. His father calls him if he doesn't wake up. He washes his hands and face. Then he has breakfast. After this, he goes to school on his bicycle.

Mary gets to school at nine o'clock in the morning. Her brother brings her when he has time. She takes out her books and pencils. Then she sits down at her desk. After this, she listens to her teacher.

6.3.2 Substitution of sentences in paragraphs using plans and outlines

The following is an example of a sentence substitution exercise involving the use of two different literary devices. In *a* the subject is stated at the start and described or developed in the rest of the paragraph. In *b* the sentences gradually build up to a climactic statement of the subject in the last sentence. These paragraphs function as frames for the substitution of new sentences.

a ¹My sister is a very generous girl. ²She often gives money to friends who have less than she has. ³In fact she is a very expensive daughter for our parents because she hardly keeps anything they give her.

b ¹I earn £85 a week and support my wife and two children with this meagre income. ²We pay £20 a week for rent, while food and clothing, without any luxuries, cost about £40 a week. ³We need another £10 for fares and entertainment, etc. ⁴This leaves £15 which is swallowed by the Taxation Department. ⁵My savings amount to the depressing sum of £0. ⁶The taxes in this country are exorbitant!

These paragraphs have numbered sentences, but they could also be displayed with each sentence in a separate column, as in a conventional frame. Students then use new sentences such as the following to slot into the right places and produce new paragraphs:

a He often gives encouragement to students who have less ability than others.

In fact he is the most popular teacher in the school because he never punishes anyone who makes a mistake.

My teacher is a very kind man.

b I work five days a week, and go to lectures on three evenings.

I cannot manage part-time studies!

This leaves one afternoon when I have to visit my grandparents.

I have no spare time at all.

I study on two evenings a week, and go to the library for one morning and two evenings.

I need one day and two evenings for shopping, washing clothes and general cleaning of my home.

Another way of displaying the model paragraphs is to demonstrate more of their structure. We can call these *plans* or outlines rather than 'substitution frames', but the principle is the same:

a

Sentence 1	Statement of topic
Sentence 2	Illustration of topic
Sentence 3	Consequence of topic

b

| Sentences 1–5 | Illustration of topic |
| Sentence 6 | Statement of topic |

Even more detail might be appropriate for some students, for instance:

a

Sentence 1	Topic—descriptive statement about one feature
Sentence 2	Exemplification—one example of the feature
Sentence 3	Consequence—one result of the feature arising from one further exemplification

b

Sentence 1	Basic fact relevant to topic
Sentences 2, 3, 4	Analysis of basic fact in Sentence 1
Sentence 5	Consequence of 2, 3, 4
Sentence 6	Implication of 5 = statement of topic

Whichever kind of plan is chosen, students are then given new sentences or merely topics that lend themselves to further paragraphs of the same kind.

The teacher might also wish to exploit the tone difference between the two original paragraphs. Whereas the first is quite colourless, the second is somewhat emotive (*meagre, luxuries, swallowed, depressing, exorbitant*). So, in making substitutions, students can be asked to replace a colourless word with a colourless word, an emotive word with an emotive one.

Even in elementary English paragraph construction can be taught by plans. The example below is from *Writing in English 1*.

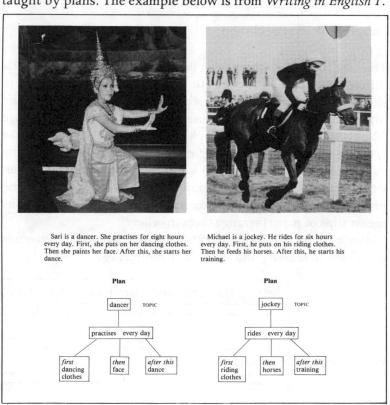

Sari is a dancer. She practises for eight hours every day. First, she puts on her dancing clothes. Then she paints her face. After this, she starts her dance.

Michael is a jockey. He rides for six hours every day. First, he puts on his riding clothes. Then he feeds his horses. After this, he starts his training.

Plan

dancer TOPIC

practises every day

| *first* dancing clothes | *then* face | *after this* dance |

Plan

jockey TOPIC

rides every day

| *first* riding clothes | *then* horses | *after this* training |

6.3.3 Substitution of paragraphs in longer pieces using plans and outlines

Yet a further way of utilising substitution is to move on to substitution in whole essays, stories, etc. For instance students can be shown an essay in three paragraphs with this conventional plan:

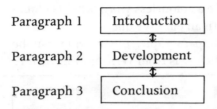

Paragraph 1 — Introduction

Paragraph 2 — Development

Paragraph 3 — Conclusion

They are then given three new, fully-written paragraphs about a different subject and asked to fit them into the same plan. There should be some indications of where each paragraph fits, eg the introductory paragraph may use a common opening (see page 52), the development paragraph may start with a phrase like 'This is seen in the following examples', and the concluding paragraph may start with 'To conclude'. Students could then either number the new paragraphs to show how they fit the plan, or write them out in the correct order, or (if the paragraphs are on slips of paper) arrange them in order.

Similar work can be done with narrative, where the pattern is often easy to identify and show in an outline, eg

Paragraph 1 — Setting the scene and introducing characters

Paragraph 2 — Event 1

Paragraph 3 — Event 2

etc — etc

The above examples are simple ones, to be used in introducing students to the method of using outlines and doing substitution. But the work can become more complex. The paragraph development of an essay could move through any one of the logical ways of presenting ideas discussed in Chapter 2, Section 2.3, and narrative can include the complexities of alternation of description and action, changes of point of view, flashbacks, etc.

7 Guided writing

7.1 General principles

Guided writing stands as a bridge between controlled and free writing. It includes any writing for which students are given assistance such as a model to follow, a plan or outline to expand from, a partly-written version with indications of how to complete it, or pictures that show a new subject to write about in the same way as something that has been read. Guided writing should be preceded by some familiarisation and controlled exercises, as was suggested in Chapter 1, page 14. It is the final step in preparing students for an attempt to write freely.

The main exercise types are Completion, Reproduction, Compression, and Transformation. Some of the suggestions that follow are closer to controlled writing, some are almost free.

7.2 Guided writing by completion

The best known completion exercise is 'filling in the blanks'. A passage is given, with selected words or phrases missing, sometimes with an indication of how many letters or words have been omitted (eg .... or - -). Students have to complete the passage. Depending on how much help the students need, the words or phrases needed for the blanks may or may not be given. If they are, the exercise is closer to controlled work; if not, it can be called guided.

Completion exercises can be used for any of the writing skills. The most obvious application is to the teaching of linking words and phrases (see Chapter 3, Section 3.3). But more complex skills can also be helped by completion exercises. For instance, to teach the logical presentation of contrast in description students can be given a paragraph with one half of the contrast missing, or to teach description of a process they can be given a paragraph with one or two stages of the process missing. (See Chapter 2, Section 2.3 for a discussion of presentation of ideas.)

7.2.1 Completion by matching

Any completion exercise can be assisted by pictures. For instance, students can match words to pictures in the blank spaces in sentences and then complete the sentences, eg

A is an instrument used in writing. It . . . . .

Picture matching can also be used for students to complete stories with missing paragraphs. Likewise, diagrams or charts can help them complete essays with missing sections, and so on.

7.2.2 Completion by multiple choice questions

Students are given three or four possible items for any blank and select the appropriate one to fill in.

7.2.3 Completion using plans and outlines

In Sections 6.3.2 and 6.3.3 it was suggested that substitution frames could be adapted as plans to show the structure of whole paragraphs. These are helpful for completion exercises. For instance, one paragraph omitted from a story or essay can be written by students following such a plan. This technique can be used for many aspects of writing, eg the alternation of dialogue and narration in a story, the steps of an argument or the logical arrangement of a description. In each case, a paragraph is omitted and students have the aid of a plan to write it and thus complete the story or essay.

7.3 Guided writing by reproduction

Reproducing a piece of writing may be *exact* reproduction of something read (or heard, on occasion) either by copying it or by re-writing it from memory, or else it may be *free* reproduction in which students re-write something 'in their own words' (even trying to improve upon the original, if they can). Free reproduction is a bridge to totally free writing.

In many of the following exercises the original passage that is to be reproduced could well be in the native language so that the reproduction would involve some 'free translation', ie conveying the same meaning but without word-for-word exactness. This is a very useful way of providing content for students who would otherwise spend more time worrying about what to write than about how to write.

In an exercise involving reproduction from memory it is a help to let students have an outline to follow.

7.3.1 Reproduction by matching

(*The numbering of exercises continues from page 92*)

50 Narration Students read or listen to a story, and then use pictures as a guide to reproducing it.

7.3.2 Reproduction by MCQs

51 Linking devices Students read a passage, then reproduce it as exactly as possible from memory by choosing from MCQs which present three possible versions of each sentence in the passage. Only one of the versions contains the correct linking word.

7.3.3 Reproduction by copying

52 Punctuation Students copy out a given passage that is unpunctuated and supply the punctuation.

53 Listening comprehension Students listen to a passage read by the teacher or on tape, and then reproduce it from memory.

7.4 Guided writing by compression

Many examinations still require *précis*, or summary writing, on the grounds that it is useful for note-taking, forces close attention to the thread of an argument, and helps separate essential from non-essential details. Whatever one's views on these matters, compression does involve *a* recognition of main points and *b* the use of paraphrase (see also Section 7.5). Both are important skills in writing.

7.4.1 Compression by underlining

54 Presentation of ideas Given a salesman's long, detailed report on a new machine, students underline key points that would be included in a preliminary letter to the manager of a company that might buy it.

55 Style Students underline those parts of a long passage that could be omitted from a summary of it.

7.4.2   Compression by outlines

56   Logical function   Given a long passage and an outline (perhaps prepared by the students themselves), students write a
summary of the main points. The outline could be in the form of
headings, a chart, a diagram, etc. See Chapter 6, Section 6.3 and
Chapter 8, Section 8.2 for examples of outlines. This exercise is
most useful when the passage clearly exemplifies one of the
logical functions described in Chapter 2, Section 2.3.

7.5   Guided writing by paraphrase

Transformation   This means the changing of a small number
of features (perhaps only one) of a piece of writing, so that it
becomes suitable for a different context, or fulfils a different
purpose within the same context. It can sometimes involve
grammatical transformation. For example a change from the
active 'I accept your advice' to the passive 'Your advice will be
accepted' can change a statement from a personal to an impersonal response.

But any other change involving vocabulary, paragraph structure, essay planning, emotive tone, etc can be included in useful
paraphrase exercises. For instance, each of the following can be
seen as a paraphrase of any of the others, and students could be
shown how each is useful for a different purpose or context.

It was struck at its uppermost point with minimum force.
He tenderly brushed against the top as gently as a mother
touching her baby's head.
He touched the top of the object with great gentleness.
He touched the top gently.
After due consideration, it was agreed to put into effect a
light stroke against the head of the object.

Mason claims he only touched the top of the thing very carefully.

He protested, 'I only touched it!'

7.5.1 Paraphrase by matching

57 *Linking words* Given a passage using *he*, students match it with a picture showing a girl involved in the same activities, and then re-write the passage changing *he* to *she* as necessary.

58 *Emotive tone* Given plain statements, students change them to suit different writers suggested by pictures. For instance, starting with the plain statement 'Be careful' and shown a picture of a mother writing to a son who is on holiday alone, students change the statement to something like 'Whatever happens, do be careful on the road'. Shown a picture of a policeman preparing a poster urging the public to take care on the roads, they change it to something like 'Pedestrians must look both ways before crossing a road.'

7.5.2 Paraphrase by comparing

59 *Paragraphs* Given two paragraphs, *a* with the topic sentence as an opening generalisation and *b* with the topic sentence as a conclusion, students transform a third passage with the topic sentence in the middle into type *a* or *b* and observe what changes in linking words are required by the change.

60 *Description* Given two different objects to describe and two contrasting passages showing different kinds of description, students choose one of the passages as a model to describe each of the objects. For instance, one model passage describes a train from one end to the other; the other model passage describes a helicopter first outside then inside. The technique of the first pas-

sage would be suitable as a model to describe a street; the second would suit a description of a car.

61 Style Students are presented with three ways of writing or reporting a dialogue:

a   Are you coming, Peter?
     Nearly ready, Barbara.
     Well, hurry, up!

b   Barbara called, 'Are you coming, Peter?' and he replied, 'Nearly ready, Barbara.' But she shouted impatiently, 'Well, hurry up!'

c   When it was time to leave, Barbara called up the stairs to see if Peter was coming. He answered that he was nearly ready. But she had been waiting for so long that she felt impatient and shouted angrily for him to hurry up.

Then, given a sample similar to any *one* of these three models, they transform it into the style of the other two.

7.5.3   Paraphrase by MCQ

62 Communicative function Given a letter of advice, students change it into a letter of warning or threat, by choosing from lists of MCQ items (words, phrases, or sentences) that could be used.

63 Style Given an informal letter, students change it into a formal one by choosing alternative words from MCQ lists.

64 Style Given a passage in a sad tone, students change it into a happy passage about the same topic (eg the writer moving from one town to another), by using words chosen from given MCQ lists.

7.5.4 Paraphrase by copying

65 Communicative function Given a sample telegram as a model, students transform a detailed message into telegram style. This assumes, of course, that preceding exercises have practised 'telegram English'.

66 Communicative function Students change a report about a machine into an advertisement for it, or *vice versa*.

67 Paragraphs Students transform a given paragraph into one with a different structure. For example, they change a paragraph starting with a generalisation followed by examples into one starting with examples and ending with a generalisation.

68 Narrative Given a model story in the simple past tense, students transform another story from present tense into simple past by copying the verb forms of the model. (The teacher must ensure that the same verbs occur in both stories.)

8 Free writing

8.1 General principles

In free writing along traditional lines students are presented with a topic and are then free to write as they please. Unfortunately this produces such a welter of unexpected errors (different ones in every composition) that it leaves the teacher with little option other than handing back a composition covered in a rash of angry red marks—most discouraging to student and teacher alike—or simply hoping that the errors will eventually disappear.

Nevertheless, the ability to write freely and independently is the undoubted goal of writing lessons. What this book has tried to show is how that goal can be reached by careful attention to the skills needed to achieve it and by careful selection of appropriate preparatory exercises. Free writing is seen as the aim of a specific set of writing exercises: 'the ability to write freely what has been taught', not 'the ability to write anything at all'. It means that the writing which has been practised under control can, at last, be accomplished without control. That is why advanced as well as elementary students need some familiarisation, controlled and guided exercises before they attempt to write freely in whatever style or variety is being taught. At all levels, students must be taught what they have to write, rather than being allowed to plunge in and left to sink or swim. That does not mean that all errors can be avoided. But they will be considerably lessened after good preparation.

As the final stage of a writing lesson, free writing is still a classroom exercise. It is not the normal free writing of everyday life. Therefore, students still need to be assisted in getting started and in organising their ideas. In real life, writing normally arises out of a genuine need to communicate something to somebody but in the classroom that need has to be created in such a way that students do not have to rack their brains for something to write about but can concentrate on the actual writing itself.

Students should learn to ask themselves certain useful questions before they start. If the cue for their work is a piece of writing, for instance, and the instruction is something like: 'Read the following and then write a similar passage (or story, essay, etc) about . . . . .', then they need to consider

1   Who wrote this?
2   Who is it written for?
3   Why did the writer write it?
4   Can I write to a similar person for a similar reason about the new topic?

If the cue is simply a topic or picture, then the students need to crystallise their ideas on the subject-matter as well as on the form their writing will take. They can start with either form or content. The questions they should ask themselves are:

A   **Content:**
1   What has this topic to do with me? How does it, or could it affect me personally?
2   What associations has the topic for me? (Here the students could do a small free association exercise, ie simply write down anything and everything that occurs to them.)
3   Who would be interested in, or likely to receive some writing about this? (It is easier to write for someone known to the writer, so, if the topic allows narrative, students could write for a younger brother or sister, or for other members of the class,

etc. For other kinds of writing, the readership might have to be imaginary, but it should be specific.)

4 Are there interesting contrasts here, eg between the topic's relevance to my early life and its relevance now, or between its interest for me and for other people?

5 What place has this in my community, ie what people, times, activities, and attitudes are associated with it?

6 Could I describe this to a man from Mars? and so on.

B Form

1 What sort of thing am I going to write—a story, a letter (what kind?), an invitation, etc?

2 What is my main aim in writing?

If students are shown how to proceed through a series of such questions, they will learn a systematic approach to writing which will considerably relieve them of the burdens of 'dreaming up' something to write.

Another useful prompt for free writing is the stimulus of some other piece which the student can react to, by either presenting a counter-argument, or giving additional views, relating a parallel experience of his own, or giving the same argument from a different point of view, and so on. The original piece would sometimes serve as a model of organisation or style, but the student could be left free if he wished to write something related but different (eg if the original was a newspaper article, he might want to react to it with a letter to the editor).

The further sections of this chapter describe other ways of assisting free writing through what can be called 'free writing exercises', namely: expansion, completion, translation, transposition, writing about pictures, writing games.

8.2 Free writing by expansion

This is the opposite of *précis* or summary writing. One method of arranging it is to give students a short passage with, say, four clearly stated main points. Students then take each point in turn and write a paragraph about each one, thus expanding the original.

Another method is to exploit some of the very common forms of information display that are widely used, for example time-tables, charts, diagrams, maps, programmes, menus, tables of contents, etc. Any of these can provide the basic information that students can expand into extended writing. If the information is from an English source, then this method has the added merit of training students to read it. On the other hand, there is no reason why information in the native language should not be used. For instance, a railway time-table in Japanese could be used to write a short account of railway times that a group of English tourists needed to know about. Again, a map of the local district could be used as the basis of a description for English readers. Likewise, bank statements, passport application forms and many other compressed information displays can be used in the native tongue as starting points in writing an informative account for English readers.

Finally, students should have some acquaintance with conventionally used ways of outlining information. Such outlines are often found in connection with chapters of textbooks or journal articles especially, but not only, in technical fields. Writers frequently use them when planning their work, and they are of great assistance in teaching students how to prepare for extended writing. The outlines on the following two pages are the most common, and should be used as soon as the teacher judges his class able to follow them. They can be the basis of single paragraphs or of whole essays.

1 Conventional numbered and lettered arrangement:

A Foreign Student in London

I LIVING CONDITIONS

   A Accommodation
       1 Standards
       2 Cost
          (i) rent
          (ii) heating, lighting, etc

   B Food
       1 Where to buy
          (i)   Supermarkets
          (ii) Small local shops
          (iii) Specialist 'foreign food' shops
       2 Restaurants

II MAKING FRIENDS

   A Other foreign students
       1 At college
          (i) on the course
          (ii) in college clubs
       2 At non-college clubs

   B Meeting the English

III STUDIES

   etc

2 TABLE

I Living conditions

Accommodation standards	Accommodation costs	Food: buying	Food: eating out

II Making friends

Other students on course	Other students at college	Non-college clubs	Meeting the English

<u>III Studies</u>
etc

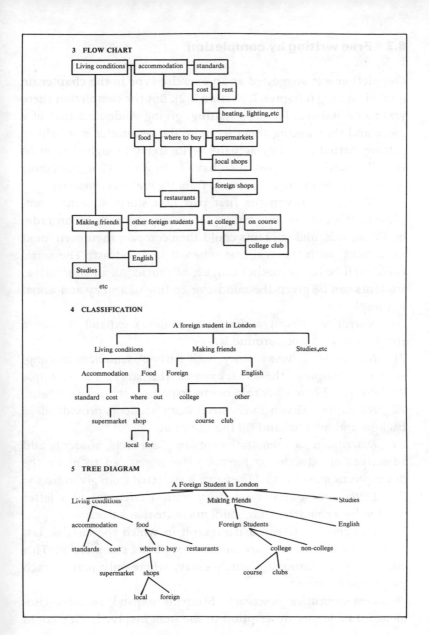

3 FLOW CHART

- Living conditions
  - accommodation — standards
    - cost — rent
      - heating, lighting, etc
  - food — where to buy — supermarkets
    - local shops
    - foreign shops
    - restaurants
- Making friends — other foreign students — at college — on course
  - college club
  - English
- Studies

etc

4 CLASSIFICATION

A foreign student in London

- Living conditions
  - Accommodation
    - standard
    - cost
  - Food
    - where
      - supermarket
      - shop
        - local
        - for
    - out
- Making friends
  - Foreign
    - college
      - course
      - club
    - other
  - English
- Studies, etc

5 TREE DIAGRAM

A Foreign Student in London

- Living conditions
  - accommodation
    - standards
    - cost
  - food
    - where to buy
      - supermarket
      - shops
        - local
        - foreign
    - restaurants
- Making friends
  - Foreign Students
    - college
      - course
      - clubs
    - non-college
  - English
- Studies

8.3 Free writing by completion

Completion was suggested as an exercise type in the chapter on guided writing (Chapter 7, Section 7.2). But the completion there was to be assisted. For free writing, giving students a part of a piece and then asking them to write the remainder is a help to getting started and they actually write freely though they must be influenced by the part they have been given. (*The numbering of the following exercises continues from the previous chapter.*)

69 Narrative   Given the first part of a story, students complete it. It would be interesting to use a serial perhaps on radio or TV for this, and students could then compare their own 'next instalment' with the real one when it is broadcast. The serial could well be in the mother tongue, of course. As an alternative, students can be given the middle or ending of a story and asked to complete it.

70 Narrative   Given a dialogue, students expand it into a story, or write a story around it.

71 Narrative   Given a story with parts of sentences missing, students complete them to expand the story, for example '(When?) . . . her mother told her to go (Where?) . . . she . . . ' etc.

72 Narrative   Given a very brief story, students provide more background material and fill the story out.

73 Description   Given statements of plain facts, students add adjectives or adverbs to improve the effects, eg to make the descriptions more vivid. (They can be selected from given lists.)

74 Letter-writing   Given a story with a reference to a letter written by a character in it, students write that letter.

75 Paragraphs   Given a paragraph in which the last, or last two or three sentences are missing, students complete it. This could be done through a whole essay, where only part of each paragraph is given.

76 Communicative functions   Students expand an advertisement into a longer description of the item involved. This could be done with a telegram or other brief form like a poster, road sign, etc.

77 *Dialogue* Given one side of a conversation, students provide the other side. (Note that providing missing questions is more challenging than providing missing answers. But not all dialogues are question-answer!)

78 *Argument* Students expand a simple presentation of a point into a persuasive argument by adding more illustrations to prove it.

8.4 Translation

This is not normally thought of as a composition exercise, but inasmuch as translation from the native language leads to the writing of whole pieces of English it has its place both as a stimulus, a source of ideas and an experience of writing which can indicate to the student that there are important similarities and differences between his native language and English. Translation for composition need not be used to focus on small points of vocabulary and grammar. The focus can, as in all the other writing exercises, be on matters relating to the writing skills. So a translation should, for the purpose of a writing exercise, be fairly free (ie not exactly word for word) and yet convey the same ideas and effect and follow the logic of the original. Pieces could be chosen to highlight specific writing skills.

Many exercises can be devised by simply adding the dimension of translation to any of the kinds of exercises previously described. For example, writing sentences or paragraphs to match series of pictures could be cued by the sentences in the native language.

8.5 Free writing by transposition

Transposition is an interesting and challenging writing exercise. For instance, students read a story set, say, in England and then try to transpose it to their own home town. They first have to isolate the theme, the main events and subsidiary details, and then decide in advance what major changes would be required for the transposition to be acceptable. They should follow the original story as closely as possible, altering only what is absolutely necessary.

They can also transpose a story from one part of a country to another (eg from city to countryside), or from one viewpoint to another (eg a doctor heroine can become a teacher hero), or from one age group to another (events involving adults change to involve children), etc. In each case, it is best if the version the students write deals with a setting that is close to them (ie the transposition should be from remote to familiar).

Transposition has the further merit that it can very effectively show cultural differences (or similarities). It should proceed in two stages to make the best use of this potential. The teacher first selects a short passage or story from a reader in English and the class looks for the words and phrases whose meaning relies on cultural values. They then consider questions like: What is the equivalent (if any) in our culture? In what respects do the two cultures differ here? How does our language differ from English because of the contrast between the two cultures? (Similarities should also be noted.)

The second stage is the re-writing of the chosen passage, to conform to the native culture of the students. Sometimes it may be found that it cannot be done. This discovery is itself of great educational value.

8.6 Free writing using pictures

A very commonly used stimulus for writing is to show a picture or strip cartoon. In fact the use of pictures is often called a 'guided writing' exercise. But pictures alone do not provide more than content. Unless help is also given with the language to be used, there is no real guidance for the actual writing.

The results of using pictures merely as stimulus are frequently very disappointing. Teachers start to wonder why apparently intelligent and competent students 'cannot even describe a picture'. They tend to leave out necessary information, or insert unnecessary details. They fail to provide links, so that their writing would not be understood without recourse to the pictures. They confuse tenses—a natural outcome of being asked, say, to write in the past tense while looking at pictures which would inspire the use of the present. And, chiefly, they approach the task in a disorganised fashion, moving at random from one item in a picture to another.

The simple fact is that students have to learn how to write from a picture. Chapter 7 discussed guided writing, and virtually any exercise there can be motivated and aided by pictures. This section discusses the use of pictures in free writing.

Sometimes a picture is used as a stimulus for a composition in the same way as a subject title. For instance a picture of a lighted cigarette might stimulate the same kind of essay as 'The dangers of smoking'. In this case, the approach to the use of the picture is the same as for free composition in general.

When a picture (or series of pictures) is used as the *focus* of writing, there are useful procedures to follow. These can be shown by considering pictures as falling into three categories: pictures of objects, of scenes, and of activities.

Although there are limitless ways in which an object (whether picture or actual thing) can be described, the learner is best helped by a simple, logical approach on which he can ring the changes at a later stage. Questions like the following help to organise students' thinking (as well as the teacher's selection of pictures):

1   What is this object?   2   How big is it?   3   What colour(s) is it?   4   What are its main parts?   5   Is it best described (i) from one end to the other; (ii) from outside to inside; (iii) from top to bottom; (iv) in a logical order of parts?   6   Who uses it?   7   Where?   8   When?   9   What for?

If the 'object' is a person or animal, the questions are slightly different: 1   Who is this person?/What animal is it?   2   How old is he/she?/Is it fully grown?   3   What country is he/she from?/Where would you see it?   4   What is his/her occupation?/What are its habits?   5   What can be deduced about character from this picture?/What disposition has this animal: wild/tame; dangerous/harmless?   6   Is the person/animal best described in terms of (i) shape, size, limbs; (ii) colour of hair, eyes, etc; (iii) clothing, etc?

In the case of a picture of a scene, questions like these are relevant: 1   What main scene is it?   2   Where is it?   3   What are the main things in it?   4   What are the main features of the main thing(s)?   5   Is it a complex scene with many details (eg a street), or is it one principal object surrounded by peripheral items (eg a house surrounded by trees, flowers, etc)?   6   If it is a complex scene, can it best be described overall first, and then with attention to detail?   7   If it is one principal object, can it best be described by starting with that object and working outwards to the peripheral details?

In the case of a picture of an activity, quite different questions apply: 1   What main event is occurring/has occurred/is going to occur?   2   What connected events are occurring/have occurred/are going to occur?   3   Who, in the picture, participates? 4 Who, not in the picture, participates? (if anyone). 5 What is the cause of, or reason for, this/these event(s)? 6 What is the result of the activity? 7 Is there a sequence of events to be narrated?

Of course, if possible, pictures should be chosen so that the writing they lead to will be of some practical interest. For example the 'composition' of two famous still-life paintings could be compared and the paintings evaluated. This would give practice in description and comparison. Or again, pictures showing events at a football match can lead to commentaries on the play. Pictures of scenic beauty-spots can be described and evaluated as illustrations for tourist brochures (eg the students pretend to be an editor accepting, or rejecting, the pictures and giving reasons). As long as the use of pictures is carefully planned, it is a very productive aid to writing practice.

Finally, the reverse process—from writing to pictures—has a complementary value, especially for younger learners. Having to draw pictures in relation to something they (or others in the class) have written, perhaps as part of a game, helps to consolidate the meaning of the writing (for example if it consists of instructions for making something like a simple machine).

8.7 Free writing in games

Games can be used as a follow-up to composition exercises, or else as a stimulus to start writing and a preliminary to further exercises. There are many books suggesting language games, and even those which are not specifically aimed towards writing can often be adapted to incorporate writing. The games suggested here can be adapted to many different teaching points and levels of English.

Alibi A small group of students invent a mystery situation involving a robbery, or other crime, and choose one or two members of the class as suspects. The group prepares a list of questions which the suspects must answer in order to clear themselves of suspicion. They write their alibis in the form of a short report.

Consequences   A large piece of paper is folded many times. The teacher writes a suggestion for a sentence in each fold, and it is then passed around the class for each student in turn to write either a word or a sentence and then fold the paper so that the next one cannot see what has been written. For instance, if the topic is 'New Year Resolutions', the teacher could write:

(name). . . . .

FOLD

promises to. . . . .

FOLD

if (name). . . . .

FOLD

agrees to. . . . .

FOLD

etc.

At the end, the whole piece is read aloud.

Families   One student who has a large family tells the class (who are not allowed to take notes) all about the members of his family, including at least three generations, using a family tree.

The students have a blank family tree in front of them and when the speaker has finished, they make notes on it. The first student to write a complete and accurate account of the family, in prose, wins.

Persuasion   Every student writes a description of a country or a town for the rest of the class to visit. When everyone has read everyone else's, there is a secret vote for the most attractive, and the writer of it is the winner.

Spot the liar!   Students are shown a series of pictures of evidence related to a crime, together with a number of statements by witnesses, one of whom can be proved a liar from some evidence in the pictures (eg a clock in the background). The first student to spot the liar, and to write a detective's report proving it, is the winner. This game could be prepared by the class to play against another class (or in teams within one class).

Picture story   Place randomly chosen pictures (about six) in no particular order on a table and let groups of three to four students write a story together, using the pictures in any order they like. When they have finished, groups can compare their stories.

Drawing   Students write a description of a non-existent animal, or machine, and give it to another student to draw.

Pictures or diagrams   Have pairs of similar pictures or diagrams in which the difference in detail would require a specific language difference, eg 'a long, narrow road' contrasted with 'a short, wide road'; 'he has thrown the ball' contrasted with 'he is going to throw the ball'; 'at the top of the diagram' contrasted with 'at the side of the diagram'. Each student choses a picture and writes a description of it. All pictures and descriptions are then laid out in mixed order on a large table and students compete to find matching pairs.

Getting to know each other   A pleasant game for the start of the year is to give students each a sheet with a series of personal questions like 'How many brothers have you got?', 'Where were you born?', etc. When all the sheets are completed they are distributed at random around the class without any names on them. Students then receive an application form to fill out, using the information they now have about another student (eg a passport application, an application for a job, etc.) When these forms have been completed students move around showing their forms to each other until everyone has found his own.

The wishing game   In pairs, students ask each other, first, 'What do you wish for?', then 'What would you do if you got it?', and then 'What would you do after that?' and this last question is repeated five times. When each member of the pair has had a turn, they use each other's replies to write a past-tense narrative *as if* the other had had his wish fulfilled. The first pair to finish wins the game.

Treasure hunt Students prepare the hunt by hiding toys, sweets, or other rewards in various places in the classroom or playground. They then write detailed instructions for finding each treasure on slips of paper. Each slip of paper is hidden in a different place and leads the seeker to the treasure. (Some slips of paper may give false instructions, some may lead finders to other slips of paper—there are various ways of making the treasure hunt take longer!) The students then call members of another class to hunt the treasure. Alternatively two teams of the same class compete.

Guessing games Descriptions of objects, people, historical events, heroes and heroines, film and stage stars, etc can be written by students and given to others to guess who or what they represent.

Glossary

Cohesion The relationships between sentences, as signalled by words, phrases, and semantic ties. *See* **Connecting words**

Communicative skills Skills needed to communicate effectively in real-life situations, the view being that competence in grammar and vocabulary alone are insufficient for genuine communication.

Connecting words Often called Linking Words. Those words and phrases which signal the relationships between sentences, eg *and, but, then, however, in addition to, on the other hand, after that, on the contrary. See* **Cohesion**.

Controlled writing Often called Controlled composition. Writing in which students follow exact instructions so as to produce correct written work, eg filling in blanks, sentence-combining, etc. Contrasts with **Guided writing** and **Free writing**.

Cue Any device used to elicit a response from students, eg pictures, music, questions, flash cards, etc.

Discourse A flow of spoken or written language, either from one speaker or writer (eg speech, essay) or involving two or more people (eg conversation). Discourse analysis is the study of how such discourse is structured, and what makes it effective as communication.

ESP English for Special Purposes, eg science, business, tourism.

Emotive tone The effect that a piece of writing (or speech) has on the recipient, eg it may evoke sympathy, or humour, or anger, etc.

Function   The purpose behind a piece of language used as communication, ie what the speaker or writer intended by expressing himself in that way. Typical functions are apologising or describing a cause-effect sequence. The former is an instance of what is called a communicative function and the latter a logical function in this book.

Functional   *See* **function.** Used in expressions like functional writing, functional teaching, functional syllabus, functional grammar, all of which emphasise the communicative approach to language.

Familiarisation   That part of teaching in which a student becomes familiar with the kind of language he is later to produce. It involves reading or listening and exercises that do not require free production of the language involved. Compare 'recognition' work in pronunciation teaching.

Free writing   Writing in which the student is given a topic but no detailed assistance.

Group work   Co-operative language practice between small groups of students (3–6 in most cases). It is not a matter of sitting together in groups, but of pooling efforts in a given task.

Guided writing   Writing in which the student has more freedom than in **Controlled writing** but less than in **Free writing**, because of assistance such as given outlines, a model to copy, etc.

Linking words   Often called Linking devices. *See* **Connecting words**.

Lexis/Lexical   Vocabulary/Related to vocabulary. Used in expressions like 'He has a good command of lexis (= vocabulary)' or 'There are lexical problems in this reading passage (= the vocabulary is too difficult)'.

Model   A piece of writing (or other language form) used to demonstrate or guide students in their own use of language.

Motivation   The incentive, or wish, to learn. Considered likely to be much increased by communicative use of language in the classroom.

Role play   A form of drama in the classroom, but without a prepared script, so that students are merely given parts, or roles, in a certain situation, and allowed to act freely.

Scheme of work   Plan or outline of what is going to be taught over a series of lessons.

Syllabus   The list of items that are to be learned during a course.

Topic sentence   The sentence in a paragraph which indicates to the reader what the main point of the writing is, ie what the writer intends to communicate. It is most frequently near the beginning of a piece of writing, but it may be delayed in order to achieve a certain amount of suspense.

Variety of writing   Used in this book to mean a specific form of writing used to fulful a specific communicative function, eg a menu, a shopping list, an invoice. (But the term *variety* is more generally used to refer to dialectal, or regional kinds of English throughout the world.)

Bibliography

(E = elementary, I = intermediate, A = advanced)

I. Books for teachers

Most books on methods of teaching English contain comments on the teaching of writing. These four have particularly useful sections:

E. D. Allen and R. M. Valette, *Classroom Techniques: Foreign Languages and English as a Second Language*, 1972, New York, Harcourt Brace Jovanowich, Inc.

J. A. Bright and G. P. McGregor, *Teaching English as a Second Language*, 1970, London, Longman.

G. Broughton, C. Brumfit, R. Flavell, P. Hill and A. Pincas, *Teaching English as a Foreign Language*, 2nd Ed. 1980, London, Routledge and Kegan Paul.

W. M. Rivers and M. S. Temperley, *A Practical Guide to the Teaching of English*, 1978, New York, Oxford University Press.

Two recent books summarise current approaches to the teaching of writing. They both contain useful book lists:

D. Byrne, *Teaching Writing*, 1979, London, Longman.

R. V. White, *Teaching Written English*, 1979, London, Allen and Unwin.

The basic text on connecting (or linking) words and devices in English is:

M. A. K. Halliday and R. Hasan, *Cohesion in English*, 1976, London, Longman.

A briefer but nevertheless useful treatment can be found in:

R. Quirk et al., *A Grammar of Contemporary English*, 1972, London, Longman; Chapter 10.

R. Quirk and S. Greenbaum, *A University Grammar of English*, 1973, London, Longman, Chapter 10.

Other helpful books are:

D. Byrne, *Teaching Oral English*, 1976, London, Longman.

J. Haycraft, *An Introduction to English Language Teaching*, 1978, London, Longman.

J. Revell, *Teaching Techniques for Communicative English*, 1981, London, Macmillan.

S. Rixon, *How to Use Games in Language Teaching*, 1981, London, Macmillan.

J. A. van Ek, *The Threshold Level for Modern Language Learning in Schools*. (Council of Europe, 1976).

II. Writing courses

A. Pincas, Series Editor, *Writing in English*, *1*, *2*, and *3*, 1982, London, Macmillan (E, I, A). A series of graded workbooks, covering a wide range of contemporary styles and topics, and using very varied guided and free exercises.

T. C. Jupp and J. Milne, *Basic Writing Skills in English*, *1980 (E)*
Guided Paragraph Writing, 1972 (I)
Guided Course in English Composition, 1969 (A)
all London, Heinemann Educational Books. All practise vocabulary and grammar, as well as composition work usually involving the use of sample paragraphs to work on.

III. Books that emphasise logical thinking and planning in writing practice.

J. Cooper, *Think and Link*, 1979, London, E. Arnold (Very A). A very interesting, but difficult, use of pictures and diagrams to promote logical organisation of ideas in writing.

M. Imhoof and H. Hudson, *From Paragraph to Essay*, 1975, London, Longman (Very A). Deals with the organisation of ideas in different kinds of paragraph.

M. Lawrence, *Writing as a Thinking Process*, 1972, Michigan, University of Michigan Press (Very A). A wide range of topics of adult interest are used to practise related vocabulary, structures and logical paragraphing.

L. Meyers, *Seeing Writing*, 1980, New York, Harcourt Brace Jovanovich (A). Very imaginative drawings as topics for writing, combined with good revision of important grammar points.

J. Moore, *Reading and Thinking in English* (4 volumes: *Concepts in Use*, *Exploring Functions*, *Discovering Discourse*, and *Discourse in Action*, graded from elementary, through intermediate, to advanced), 1979, London, Oxford University Press. Exercises in the organisation of ideas, mainly for descriptive and expository writing in science, but could be of interest to older, general students.

IV. General exercise books for practice of writing.

J. Arnold and J. Harmer, *Advanced Writing Skills*, 1978, London, Longman (A). Relates writing to numerous different functions and topics of everyday life, backed up with vocabulary and grammar practice, and visual materials.

R. G. Bander, *American English Rhetoric*, 1978, New York, Holt, Rinehart and Winston (I and A). A very long and comprehensive book practising numerous different styles, functions and topics, with some grammar and vocabulary assistance, sections on punctuation and spelling, numerous model passages and essays, and many suggestions for further writing.

L. L. Blanton, *Elementary Composition Practice*, 1978, Rowley, Mass., Newbury House (E). A large book with large print and drawings, but few (though clearly set out) exercises on basic grammar points related to the writing of very short paragraphs.

D. Byrne and S. Holden, *Follow it Through*, 1978, London, Longman (A). Writing exercises set in a story that continues throughout the book. Includes a wide range of varieties, eg telegrams, reports, letters, diaries, etc. Original.

F. Chaplen, *Paragraph Writing*, 1970, London, Oxford University Press (A). Also Teachers' Book. Uses model paragraphs and gives useful notes on grammar and style. Good range of topics and types of paragraph.

R. B. Heath, *Impact Assignments in English*, 1978, London, Longmans (Very A). A good range of interesting topics and suggestions for essay writing.

J. B. Heaton, *Elementary Composition through Pictures*, 1977 (E), *Composition through Pictures*, 1966 (I),
both London, Longman. Clear drawings of common activities, followed by standard, traditional structure exercises, leading to writing a simple story.

L. A. Hill, *Writing for a Purpose*, 1978, London, Oxford University Press (I). Pictures to stimulate writing in a range of styles and functions, but very little guidance apart from vocabulary lists.

T. and S. Hodlin, *Writing Letters in English*, 1979, London, Oxford University Press (A). Very practical advice on personal and official style in letters, with useful exercises.

V. Horn, *Composition Steps*, 1977, Rowley, Mass., U.S.A. Newbury House (I). Also Teachers' Manual. A large, comprehensive book covering different styles and functions, with exercises on key grammar points, spelling and punctuation.

S. Kanelli, *Advanced English Composition*, 1977, London, Evans (A). Passages showing different styles and practising paragraphs, and linking words.

S. Menne, *Writing for Effect*, 1980, London, Oxford University Press (A). Also a Teachers' Book. The only book dealing with choice of words for effect, and various stylistic devices. Uses good sample material and clear exercises.

K. W. Moody, *Frames for Written English*, 1974, London, Oxford University Press (I). A series of short stories needing completion at certain points. Students write them out choosing from given alternative words and phrases to complete them.

R. Ridout, *Write Now*, 1975, London, Longman (E). Pre-composition work stimulated by a wide variety of pictures, diagrams, puzzles, etc.

B. J. Thomas, *Practical Information*, 1977, London, E. Arnold (A). Comprehension and composition work based on materials from a wide range of everyday situations, eg timetables, advertisements, official forms etc.

T. Zinkin, *Write Right*, 1980, London, Pergamon (A). Discussion and exercises dealing with letters, note-taking, minutes, indexing, glossary writing, etc.

V. Books providing interesting reading material that can be used for composition work devised by the teacher.

D. Byrne, *Functional Comprehension*, 1977, London, Longmans (E-I).

E. F. Candlin, *English in Style*, 1978, London, Hodder & Stoughton (I-A). Also Teachers' Book.

A. Doff and C. Jones, *Feelings*, 1980, London, Cambridge University Press (A).

A. Duff, *That's Life!*, 1979, London, Cambridge University Press (A).

A. Duff and A. Maley, *Words!*, 1978, Cambridge University Press (A).

A. Duff and A. Maley, *Variations on a Theme*, 1978, Cambridge University Press (I-A).

F. Heyworth, *The Language of Discussion*, 1978, London, Hodder & Stoughton (A).

A. Lesley, *Written English Today*, 1971, London, Macmillan (A).

A. Levine, *Penguin English Reader*, 1971, London, Penguin Books
   (A).
M. Swan, *Kaleidoscope*, and *Spectrum*,
   both 1978, Cambridge University Press (A).

Index

argument 9, 42–43, 63–65, 104
authentic materials, *see* materials
chart, Varieties of English 3
cohesion/cohesive links 55–62, *see also* linking words
common core 66
communication 2, 4, 26–44
communicative writing 23, 32–33
composition, skill of 2, 4, 26, 45–62
conjunction (cohesion) 57
connecting words, *see* cohesion and linking words
context 30
contrasts, writing about 41, 47–49
controlled writing 14, 18–20, 46, 59, 74, 91–101
correction 22–23, 110, *see also* errors
course planning 5–13
creative writing 76
cues 76, 80, 111
cultural differences 51, 118
description/descriptive writing 9, 11, 36–38, 50–51, 63–64, 104, 121
diagrams, use of 47, 87, 103, 113
dialogue 67, 104, 116, 117, *see also* speech
dictionary, use of 12
elementary writing 2, 8–9, 17, 30–32, 43–44, 49, 54, 59, 64, *see also* grading
ellipsis (cohesion) 58
emotive tone 69–71
endings for essays 52–53
errors 18, 23, 110, *see also* correction
exercises, types of 74–77

exposition/expository writing 8, 11, 63–64
familiarisation 14–18, 78–90
formality 64–68
free writing 22–23, 24, 104, 110–124
functions, communicative 2, 28–29, 84
functions, logical 36–44, 51, 54, 63–64, 103
games 5, 30, 32, 70, 121–124
grading 8–9, 27, 54, 74, 76, *see also* level
grammar and writing 2, 4, 7, 14, 27, 29, 32–33, 45, 66
group work 5, 30–31, 70
guided writing 14, 18–21, 46, 74, 94, 102–109
imitation 24, 93
instructions, the writing of 79, 81
integration of writing into course 5–13
language course and writing 5–13
lesson planning 4, 13–24
letters 30–31
level of learners 4, 27, 110, *see also* grading
lexical relationships (cohesion) 58
linking words (devices) 18, 51, 55–62, 80, 103
logical functions 36–44, 51, 54, 63–64, 103,
materials 4–5, 8, 12, 28–29, 32, 67, 70
models for writing 13, 14, 17, 18, 24, 34, 54, 93–94, 112
mother tongue 4, 23, 76, 80, 113, 117
motivation 4–5, 30
narrative 38–39, 63–65, 100, 104

native language, *see* mother tongue
notions 29
objectives 2–4, 26–27, 110
openings for essays 52
outlines, use of 54, 100, 113–115
paragraphs, paragraph plans 12–13, 17, 18, 50–55, 89, 96–101
pictures, use of 49, 80, 92, 103–104, 119–121, 123
practice (stage of lesson) 14
précis 88, 105
presentation (stage of lesson) 14
presenting ideas 36–44, 51, 54, 80
production (stage of lesson) 14
projects, use of 33
reader, awareness of 30, 51, 69, 111–112
reading 15, 24, 78, 79
sentences 9, 45–49, 53–54, 59, 94–96
speech, compared with writing 9, 66, 78, *see also* dialogue
style 4, 26, 28, 63–71

structures, *see* grammar
subject-matter 32–35, 81
substitution (cohesion) 57
substitution (exercise) 91, 93–101
summary writing 88, 105
supplementary work 7, 12–13, 74
tables, use of 47, 80, 113
teaching method 13–24, 46, 54
topic sentence 52, 54, 88
topics for writing 36–43, 111–112
traditional composition teaching 2, 4, 23, 32, 110
translation 117
varieties of written English 3, 7, 28, 32, 67, 86
vocabulary 2, 4, 7, 9–12, 13, 27, 29, 32–33, 66
writing exercises 7, 78–124
writing skills 2, 7, 23, 26–71, *see also* communication, composition, style
young learners 4